PUFFIN BOOKS

SPRING BEGINS IN MARCH

Jean Little is an award-winning author who has written more than twenty books for children, including *Different Dragons, Lost and Found, Once Upon a Golden Apple*, and two memoirs, *Little by Little* and *Stars Come Out Within*. Her books have been translated into French, German, Dutch, Danish, Greek, Japanese, and Braille. *Spring Begins in March* was originally published by Little, Brown and Company in 1966.

Ms Little lives and works near Elora, Ontario.

Jean Little

Spring Begins
In March

Puffin Books

PUFFIN BOOKS

Published by the Penguin Group

Penguin Books Canada Ltd, 10 Alcorn Avenue, Toronto,
Ontario, Canada M4V 3B2

Penguin Books Ltd, 27 Wrights Lane, London W8 5TZ, England

Penguin Books USA Inc., 375 Hudson Street, New York,
New York 10014, U.S.A.

Penguin Books Australia Ltd, 182-190 Wairau Road,
Auckland 10, New Zealand

Penguin Books Ltd, Registered Offices: Harmondsworth,
Middlesex, England

First published by Little, Brown & Company (Canada) Limited
Published in Puffin Books, 1996
Text copyright © Jean Little, 1966
3 5 7 9 10 8 6 4 2

All rights reserved.

*Publisher's note: This book is a work of fiction. Names, characters, places
and incidents either are the product of the author's imagination or are
used fictitiously, and any resemblance to actual persons living or dead,
events, or locales is entirely coincidental.*

Manufactured in Canada

Canadian Cataloguing in Publication Data

Little, Jean, 1932-
Spring begins in March

ISBN 0-14-038084-1

I. Title
PS8523.I77S67 1996   jC813'.54   C95-932147-0
PZ7.L57Sp 1996

Except in the United States of America, this book is sold subject to the
condition that it shall not, by way of trade or otherwise, be lent, re-sold,
hired out, or otherwise circulated without the publisher's prior consent in
any form of binding or cover other than that in which it is published and
without a similar condition including this condition being imposed on the
subsequent purchaser.

Visit Penguin Canada's web site at **www.penguin.ca**

To Patsy who turned into Meg
and
To Meg who turned into Maggie

Contents

1
Two Promises

MEG COPELAND hated having her hair washed.

"My back hurts," she complained.

She knew exactly what Mother would say— and Mother said it.

"If you'd stay still, Meg, we could be finished in two shakes of a dead lamb's tail."

"Ha!" Meg muttered.

She squirmed under Mother's firm hands. Then, suddenly, she reared up and grabbed for a towel.

"You got soap in my eye!" she accused, mopping her face frantically.

"I'm sorry," Mother said.

The words were polite enough, but something in Mother's voice made Meg long to stamp her foot. Instead, she dawdled, rubbing at her eye again as though it still stung, going on to fold the towel neatly and drape it over the rack, spending an extra moment adjusting it so that the ends were exactly even.

All at once, Mother's hand closed on the back of Meg's neck and pushed her head back into the basin.

"Enough is enough, Margaret Ann," she said as she rubbed in shampoo. Meg's eyes were squeezed tightly shut. She felt as though Mother were removing her scalp. She was quiet for less than a minute.

"Aren't we finished YET?" she demanded.

This time, Mother did not bother answering. She knew that Meg was well aware that they had not even started rinsing.

"Oo-ooh!" Meg ground out between shut teeth as water sloshed into her left ear.

Mother was whistling softly. Meg recognized the tune at once.

Some think the world is made for fun and frolic,
   And so do I! And so do I...

She enjoys it, Meg thought darkly. She enjoys torturing her own children.

Then she remembered the time, last summer, when Grandma Kent had offered to wash her hair. It had been a grim business. When Meg had complained about stooping over the basin, Grandma had grown flustered and let her rest.

It had taken ages. There had been no laughter, no snatch of song, no playing Twenty Questions. Meg had suggested the game but Grandma could not keep her mind on two things at once.

"It just needs rinsing now," Mother announced.

She gasped with surprise when, in reply, Meg straightened up suddenly, flung both arms around her waist and gave her a bone-crushing hug. Lather flew, spattering the tile floor. Mother pretended not to notice. She hugged her small wet daughter warmly in return.

But Meg herself noticed. She pulled away and turned back to the basin, a scowl clouding her face.

"How about Twenty Questions?" Mother suggested gently, turning on the rinse water.

"I can't think of anything," Meg growled.

Mother sighed. Wherever Meg went, whatever she did, she seemed to meet that same sigh lately. She ducked her head hastily into the water, so hastily that more splashed out onto the floor. Mother quietly went ahead with the rinsing. Meg brooded.

"There's the phone," Mother said. "I'll be right back."

Meg wrung the water out of her hair. Then she stood on her toes and examined herself in the mirror on the door of the medicine cabinet.

She made faces at herself, frowning horribly and then stretching her mouth in an elastic grin and goggling her eyes.

"Hazel eyes," Mother called them, but they were really just plain speckled. Green with brown specks or brown with green specks...

The water had darkened her hair, but when it dried, it would be more red than brown. When she was small, it had been much fairer and she could still remember the way it had clung to Mother's fingers and made soft curls. Now there was only a faint wave left, although even that was more than her sister Sally had.

Meg pulled her wet hair down over her forehead in bangs like Sally's. It hung into her eyes, which Sally's did not, but that was not important. Peering out from beneath the wet locks, Meg tried to put on a "big sister" face. She pulled the corners of her mouth down and bunched up her eyebrows until she looked thoroughly unpleasant.

"That Meg is a big bother to me," she said crossly.

"What on earth are you doing?"

Mother's question caught Meg off guard. She blinked, straightened out her features, and tried to think of an answer which made sense. But Mother did not wait. She had a dozen things to get done before supper. In an instant, Meg's head was back in the rinse water. As

4

Mother poured a pitcher of hot water over her head, Meg had no choice but to keep her eyes and mouth tightly closed.

But her thoughts were not silenced.

"I can't even have a little fun," she grumbled, inside her head. "Whatever I do, somebody doesn't like it."

Sal was forever storming, "How can I keep our room tidy if Meg drops her junk all over it the moment I get it clean?" Miss Armstrong had sighed, more than once, "Meg, your marks will never improve unless you stop dreaming and start paying attention." When Grandma Kent came to stay, she never stopped complaining about Meg's behavior. According to Grandma, Meg was a picky eater and a door-slammer and saucy and "too fond of her own way." And just before Christmas, when Meg had pushed her report card into her father's hand and then streaked away to the room she and Sal shared, she had not escaped in time to miss the tired note in Dad's voice as he asked, "Emily, how are we failing her? Things seem to be going from bad to worse."

They had been trying to pin her down to a talk about school ever since.

"It's your turn for Twenty Questions," she told her mother suddenly.

"But we're all finished," Mother said—and pulled out the plug.

5

She began to dry Meg's hair briskly with a big, rough towel. Meg was half smothered, but she liked it.

All at once, Mother put the towel aside and looked at her daughter, whose hair now stood out in a tangled bush.

"I have some news for you, Miss Margaret Ann Copeland," she said.

"What?"

Mother opened her mouth to speak and then paused. Her eyes slid away from Meg's. She scrunched up one corner of the towel in her hand and stared down at it as though it had suddenly become significant.

"What news?" Meg prodded.

"We've decided to let Sally move in with Melinda."

The words shot out of Mother in such a rush that Meg did not understand for a moment. Then she gasped and her own words erupted.

"You mean I'll have my own room? I won't have to share with Sally?"

Mother reached out and vainly tried to smooth back the tangled hair. She was smiling now at the eagerness in Meg's thin face which would, someday, be very like her own.

"Have you minded sharing so much?"

"Oh, she's always picking on me." Meg brushed aside the question. "But Mother, when will she move out? Is she going tonight?"

Mother looked horrified at the thought.

"Darling, please, not so fast! We planned to make it an extra birthday present for you. Sal can move out officially on Friday, and when you wake up a year older, you'll be in your own room. Does that suit you?"

Meg did not need to count the days till her birthday. Today was Tuesday, New Year's Day. Her birthday would arrive three weeks from Saturday. Twenty-five and one-quarter days to go! But when that day came, and Meg was old enough to know that it actually would come in time, she, Meg Copeland, would have a room to herself. She beamed at her mother.

Mother looked troubled.

"Meg," she began, speaking slowly as though she did not enjoy having to say these words, "you must understand that this is not a reward for good behavior. Your father and I are deeply worried about you. We've tried and tried to talk with you about whatever is wrong at school, but we never seem to get through to each other…"

The brightness drained out of Meg's face, as though someone had snuffed a candle. She bent her arm suddenly and began examining her elbow. Then she started to scratch it.

Mother took a deep breath and kept going.

"I know you've never had a good desk. There hasn't been room in there for two, but now, with Sal's out of the way, we thought we'd get you one of your own."

"I have a new wart," Meg muttered, pointing her elbow at Mother.

"It's invisible then," Mother said, glancing at the spot which Meg had reddened with her scratching. "Leave that alone, Meg, and LISTEN!"

Meg let her arm fall back to her side and stood like a post. Her mother went on doggedly for a minute longer.

"When you have a room of your own and a good desk, we expect you to make a fresh start at home and at school. If you'd just try..."

Her voice died away. It was no use. Meg was so clearly not listening. Her face had grown dull, even stupid. Her eyes were glazed. They looked like windows with the blinds pulled down. Her mother could not see in.

"Meg," she said sharply. She put her hand under her daughter's chin, tipped her face up and tried to meet her gaze squarely.

"Yes," Meg answered from somewhere out of reach.

"Go and get your comb and brush," Mother ordered.

Meg came out from behind the blankness. She screwed up her eyes as though the light surprised her, as though, for an instant, she had lost track of where she was. Then she swept Mother a bow.

"Madam, I rush to do thy bidding," she grinned—and pranced out of the room making as much noise as a sturdy pony.

Meg, from the time she had learned to talk, had been the family clown. The older children bickered among themselves, but Meg had arrived when they were old enough to appreciate her. Even Kent was four years her senior. "Tagalong Maggie" they had called her. It had been a nickname born mostly of love. So many family jokes had started with Meg.

Once, when she was not quite four, she had remarked in a small, cozy voice, "God was talking to me this morning."

"What did He say?" the Copelands had demanded.

"He said 'Hello' and I said 'Hello.'"

"And what happened then?" Mindy prompted.

"Then He went back up," Meg told them.

She had loved make-believe.

"I'm a mother rabbit and I've come to call," she had remarked one afternoon.

"Where are your children, Mrs. Rabbit?" her mother had inquired.

"I left them at home with a dependable baby-sitter," replied Meg calmly. "I gave her this telephone number in case of 'mergencies," she had added.

There had been so many of these treasured moments when Meg was small. They had chuckled at her quaint ways, and Meg, not always understanding the joke, had still laughed happily with them. But her first teacher had not known what to do with a clown in the class. Meg had been punished for "being bold." Little by little, she had learned to hold her tongue. Little by little, she had come to hate school. The teacher, certain that Meg was "impudent" and "badly spoiled," seldom called on her in class. Soon the little girl had learned the knack of dreaming the hours away. She had had other teachers since, but no one had managed to teach her not to waste time. Miss Armstrong had already warned the Copelands that Meg would, almost certainly, not be promoted this time.

"Growing pains," Mother comforted herself. "She'll come through all right in the end."

The front door opened. It was Sal. Melinda closed the door quickly but gently. Kent never failed to give it a good slam. Sally took a minute getting herself and her crutches in, turning around, getting balanced and then pushing the door shut. There. She had it closed now.

"Anybody home?" Sal called.

"Coming," her mother answered, going to help her daughter sweep the snow off her boots. By the time she got there, however, Sally was wielding the broom herself. She had to prop herself against the wall to do it and she was not quick or skillful but she was getting the job done, in spite of her West Highland terrier, Susie, who was bounding around her in an ecstasy of welcome.

Mother did not offer to help. Until Sally was Meg's age, she had attended a special school for crippled children where she could get the therapy and special teaching she had needed. Then a treatment center had opened in Riverside and the Copelands had brought Sally home to stay. It had been hard, at first, making Sal do things without help, but in time the whole family had come to understand that Sal's future happiness depended on her learning to do as much as she could for herself. Although she would never run freely as the others did, never, in fact, manage without some support, she had been helped by therapy and by surgery until now, she no longer needed to wear her old cumbersome leg braces and had even graduated to wrist crutches. Wrist crutches were really glorified canes. The only real difference was the "bracelet" of aluminum which fitted around Sal's wrists and left her hands free when she needed them. She had been using the wrist crutches for a year now and, although she was more unsteady than on the underarm ones, she delighted in the convenience and lightness of the shorter "sticks," as she laughingly called them.

Meg came charging through the hall at that moment, singing at the top of her lungs.

> *A room of my own!*
> *A room of my own!*
> *Heigh-ho, the derry-o,*
> *A room of my own!*

Sal put the broom back and reached for her crutches.

"I see you've told her the glad news," she said to her mother, as Meg stopped for breath. There was a hard, hurt note in her voice as she turned on her younger sister. "Why don't you at least try to sing in tune?"

"I can sing any way I want to," Meg answered back, hearing only the hardness.

She took a deep breath, getting ready to begin again, when Mother stopped her with a hand on her shoulder.

"She's just happy," she told Sal.

"You call it being 'happy.' I call it making a racket," Sal said, sitting down on the hall bench and starting to wrestle with her boots.

Emily Copeland wanted to knock their heads together. They were forever wounding each other, these two daughters of hers. She wondered how long it would be before they discovered how deep the love between them really was. The household would certainly be more peaceful, once they were separated. Yet their parents knew that they needed to find each other. Perhaps they should have left them together...

Suddenly, Mother caught sight of Meg's empty hands.

"Where are your comb and brush, young lady?"

"Oh... I guess I forgot," Meg said airily.

Her shoulders were taken in two iron hands. Mother did not raise her voice, but she gave her daughter a little shake with each terse sentence.

"Go and get your comb and brush. Do not sing on the way. Come straight back. I'll be waiting in the bathroom. Hurry."

Mother was combing out the last tangle when Meg twisted around to look at her. There was such intensity in her face that her mother paused with the brush in mid-air.

"Mother, promise me I can have a room of my own."

"But I already told you..."

"Yes, but promise!" Meg insisted.

"How about you promising to work harder in school?" Mother returned, suddenly every bit as serious as Meg herself.

There was a moment of silence. Meg had heard this time. She made a face. Then she said slowly, "Okay. I'll promise if you will."

"I promise, darling," Emily Copeland said.

2
Charlotte

"SCHOOL TOMORROW, Emily," Dad said at supper on Wednesday. "Just think of it! Peace again."

Melinda, Sally and Kent groaned, but Meg's face brightened.

"I can hardly wait," she announced.

Her brother and sisters stared at her. None of them had ever brought home a report card as bad as Meg's. Sally was beginning to have a hard time keeping up with her class now that she was in high school, but so far, even she was still passing in all her subjects. What had come over Meg?

"She must be coming down with something," Melinda decided, studying the youngest Copeland.

"School, Meg! He's talking about 'school'!" Kent pointed out.

"The other day you said you wished it would

burn down during the holidays," Sal put in.

Meg turned sullen under their combined inspection.

"Go jump in the lake," she growled.

"Easy does it, Margaret Ann," Mother warned. Then she turned on the rest. "Leave her alone. You should all be glad to go back to school. It's a privilege."

Mother went on about how fortunate they were to be able to get an education, but Meg was thinking of Charlotte. Charlotte was her only reason for being glad school began tomorrow. They had not seen each other since Charlotte left to spend the holidays with her father in Toronto. They were best friends, she and Charlotte, although it was hard to imagine two girls more different.

"I don't understand what you see in each other," Sal had said once. "You're so dreamy and Charlotte so...so..."

"What?" Meg demanded.

"Dashing!" Sal decided.

Meg raced to school on Thursday morning. As she came puffing into the playground, she saw Charlotte ahead of her, disappearing into the building.

"Charlotte!" she yelled. "Wait for me! I've something to tell you."

Charlotte Russell was a chunky girl, much taller and broader than Meg. She had round

apple cheeks, eyes so blue they glowed, a
turned-up nose and a mane of very fair hair.
When her mother was home and Charlotte's
hair was combed properly, it fell in a silver
waterfall as shimmering as Alice's in
Wonderland, and Meg was openly jealous of it.
But Mrs. Russell was usually off to work before
her daughter got up, and Charlotte, left to herself, had not the patience to fight with tangles
and find a hair-band to match her clothes.
Today, Charlotte had hauled it back and put an
elastic around it. It bobbed behind her like a
real horse's tail.

"Charlotte!" Meg called again.

Charlotte turned and tried to stand her
ground, but in spite of her square build, an
onrush of boys and girls carried her through
the door and down the hall. She and Meg did
not reach each other until they were outside
their own classroom door.

"I've something to tell you," Meg panted.

"Wait till you hear what I have to tell you,"
Charlotte countered.

A gang of boys came storming down the hall.
Meg, small for her age and thin as a twig, was
almost swept away. Charlotte dove to the rescue. She knocked several boys sideways,
grabbed at Meg's elbow, and yanked her into
the safety of the classroom.

Meg was caught off balance. She staggered

wildly, flung her arms wide to save herself, and
let go of her new pencil box. It hit the floor with
a bang. Pencils, erasers, a plastic ruler and two
marbles spilled out and rolled in a dozen different directions.

Meg reddened with embarrassment, but
Charlotte was delighted. She loved excitement.

"I'll get them," she whooped, thudding down
on her knees and scrambling after one of the
pencils which had lodged behind Miss
Armstrong's wastebasket.

Miss Armstrong covered her ears with her
hands.

"Charlotte, *please!*" she begged.

"Yes, Miss Armstrong," Charlotte returned,
not lowering her voice one whit. She grabbed
the last pink eraser from between Meg's feet
and jumped up. Stuffing everything into the
box, she thrust it into Meg's hand. Meg was not
ready and Charlotte let go too soon. It all
crashed onto the floor again.

Now Meg was scarlet with humiliation, but
Charlotte laughed aloud and plunged after the
things once more.

"You two!" Miss Armstrong said helplessly.
Meg, her eyes lowered, missed the teacher's
quick smile. "Hurry up, Charlotte. The bell is
due to ring any minute and you're right smack
in the way there."

"Yes, Miss Armstrong," Charlotte said again,

not the least bit worried. She rose for the second time, and holding onto the pencil box herself, she led the way to their desks.

"She's an old goat!" she whispered to Meg as they slid into their seats.

Meg gasped and looked hurriedly at the teacher, but she was busy at her desk and gave no sign of having heard.

"Hey!" Charlotte's voice grew loud again. "Look what my father gave me!"

Meg looked. Her eyes widened. Charlotte was wearing a new, very grown-up watch. It was small and golden and seemed too fragile on Charlotte's broad wrist.

"Mother said it was too old and she put it away in her jewel box, but I got it back out after she left for work," Charlotte said complacently. "Why not?" she went on, answering Meg's shocked eyes. "It's mine, isn't it? If your father gives you something to wear, you should be able to wear it."

Meg had long since learned not to argue with Charlotte, but still, she knew Charlotte was wrong. She tried to imagine herself going into her mother's things to get something which Mother had forbidden her to wear. It was unthinkable. Once again, she was faced by the puzzle that was Charlotte and Charlotte's family.

Mr. Russell did not live at home. Once, Meg

had asked Charlotte if her mother and father were divorced.

"Of course not," Charlotte had said. She had turned her back on Meg as she spoke and started fiddling with something on her dresser. That was not like Charlotte. "They're just separated."

"Separated?" Meg had echoed, not understanding.

Charlotte had whirled around then, her eyes fierce.

"Yes, separated," she had snapped. "Anything else you'd like to know, Miss Nosy?"

Meg had shaken her head, and she had not questioned her friend about it again. But she had never stopped working to put the pieces of Charlotte's world together tidily in her mind. She wanted to know how it felt to be Charlotte, but in spite of a clue here and a clue there, she was still bewildered by the Russells.

Mrs. Russell had a full-time job in a factory and often worked nights as a part-time waitress. Although the two girls had been friends for over a year, Meg had not seen Charlotte's mother often.

"I feel sorry for Charlotte with a mother like that," Meg had told her own mother not long before.

Mother had surprised her.

"I feel sorry for Mrs. Russell," she had replied sharply. "She has her parents to support as well as Charlotte and herself. Louise has had more than her share of troubles. When you're older, you'll understand."

Just the same, whenever Meg went home with Charlotte after school and they let themselves into the empty apartment with Charlotte's key, Meg remembered Mother waiting at home and she felt sorry, although she knew better than to let Charlotte guess.

"Hey, Meg!" Charlotte's stage whisper cut through her thoughts. "What were you going to tell me?"

Meg came back to the present with a jerk.

"Oh…" she began eagerly—and the bell rang.

That bell was the signal for silence. But Meg could not wait.

"I'm going to have a room of my own," she hissed across the aisle.

Charlotte looked as though she had expected something much more exciting. She had had a room to herself ever since she could remember. More than once, she had envied Meg having a sister to talk to at night. But Meg's shining eyes made it clear that, to her, this was terribly important.

"No kidding!" Charlotte said obligingly, right out loud.

Miss Armstrong stood up and glared down the room at Charlotte.

"One more sound out of you, Charlotte

Russell," she warned crisply, "and I'll separate you and Meg for a week!"

She meant it. She had done it several times before now. More than once, she had threatened to put them on opposite sides of the room permanently, but although their work was poor when they were together, it was impossible when they were apart. Night after night, Miss Armstrong kept them in—for entirely different reasons. Charlotte had to correct the countless errors she made as she slapdashed through her work at top speed. She was usually the first one in the class to finish an assignment. Meg stayed in to complete those self-same assignments which the rest of the class finished easily during daily work periods.

"If you two would just rub off on each other," the teacher had told them late one afternoon. "Then Charlotte might manage to work more carefully and you, Meg, more quickly."

Meg looked over and saw that Charlotte was busy admiring her new watch from every angle. Suddenly, the ceiling lights were caught and mirrored in the crystal. Charlotte turned her arms again, now watching the tiny reflection dancing along the near wall. Meg watched it dip and swoop across the blackboard. It slid along the floor next, bounded across Miss Armstrong's desk, and then skittered across the front of Miss Armstrong's skirt.

Meg held her breath in horror and fascination as Charlotte deliberately made the watch crystal throw light directly into the teacher's eyes. A flash! Miss Armstrong blinked and moved her head. Charlotte grinned. Then she tried it again.

"All right, Charlotte," Miss Armstrong said quietly. "Bring me that watch."

Charlotte argued hotly. Charlotte always argued.

"That girl would talk back to the Queen," Kent maintained.

Miss Armstrong did not bother answering Charlotte's points. She waited, with her hand out. Finally, even Charlotte ran out of words. She wrenched the watch from her wrist, stomped up the aisle, and plunked it into the outstretched palm.

Miss Armstrong put it away in her desk drawer. Charlotte tossed her head defiantly as she returned to her seat. Losing was something Charlotte did badly. Meg ducked her head over her book and pretended to be hard at work.

But although she should have been working, she was thinking instead, and not about schoolwork. She was still puzzling over the Russells. Mr. Russell gave Charlotte presents, but he never remembered her birthday. Meg did not bother trying to imagine what it would be like to have her birthday come and her father forget about it. Such a thing would never happen. And the presents themselves were different! The Copeland children got books and clothes and games, skates, doll furniture, a bicycle. Last year, Meg had been surprised when Dad had given her a globe—but not too surprised. The gifts which Charlotte received astonished her.

Meg chewed on her pencil as she listed off those she remembered. French perfume with an atomizer, a manicure set with six shades of nail polish, a gigantic panda bear much too heavy to play with, a transistor radio with a luminous dial, a black wallet with rhinestones on the front and pictures of movie stars inside, three pairs of sheer, seamless nylons, and once, earrings for pierced ears.

Charlotte demanded to have her ears pierced, but she admitted afterwards to Meg she was relieved when her mother firmly refused to let her.

What fun they had had with the nail polish, though! Mother had removed Meg's from both fingers and toes as soon as she got home, but Charlotte had gone on wearing hers long after it was chipped and peeling.

"Meg," Miss Armstrong said, "don't just cuddle the book. *Read* it. The others have almost finished."

Meg returned to the classroom with a jolt. She was behind again. She could not understand it. They had only just started a moment ago...

Miss Armstrong turned to put some work on the board. Quick as a wink, Charlotte stuck out her tongue at the teacher's back. She sent Meg a grin of victory and was deep in her book again by the time Miss Armstrong faced them once more.

"The Russells are different but they're interesting," Meg told herself stoutly. She wished that she were more like Charlotte, quick and brave and sure of herself...

Then suddenly, miraculously, Meg remembered her room.

Her pencil, which had slowly and painstakingly written *There are many different climates*, stopped moving.

I'll have my own desk, she reminded herself, exultantly. I'll study so hard Mother will be flabbergasted. I'll get a hundred in everything.

"Denise, please collect the papers now," Miss Armstrong said.

Meg looked at her one unfinished sentence. She saw, out of the corner of her eye, that Charlotte had filled two pages. She also saw that Charlotte's words were scrawled, that one whole line had been stroked out blackly, that there were at least three blots.

Both she and Charlotte would have to stay late tonight. Meg was not surprised, but her shoulders drooped and she did not hear Miss Armstrong as she gave out the next assignment.

3
Long Distance Calling

MEG HERSELF answered the phone when it rang that Saturday morning.

A moment before, she had been sprawled on her bed trying to make Sally and her friend Elsje Jansen talk to her. Since their first meeting, Meg had known that Elsje was someone special.

That Halloween night, five years ago, Meg had flung open the front door and discovered Elsje, with Libby Reeves behind her, standing on the front step. Meg still remembered how Sal had stood very still, staring at the two girls. She had tried hard to pretend she had chosen to stay in on Halloween night, but her voice had been brittle with strain as she spoke to them. Then Elsje had marched into the house, her witch's hat very straight on her head, her broomstick held firmly beneath her arm. And she and Libby had invented a costume for Sal and taken her away with them. Later, Elsje had run a dog training school in the Copelands' yard. Meg had sat cross-legged on the grass, watching the Pooch Academy in action, and had been deeply impressed by Elsje's clear tones of command. Later still, and most exciting of all, Sally and her friends had planned a surprise Saint Nicholas Feast for Elsje when she had measles. Meg had had to watch from the car, but she had seen them put the wooden shoes in front of the Jansens' door, fill them with presents, ring the bell and race away to hide themselves. She could still see the door opening, the light spilling out into the December darkness, and then hear Elsje's excited shriek, "SAINT NICHOLAS!... MOTHER! FATHER, PIET!"

"Meg, don't feel you have to stay and keep us company," Sal said too sweetly. "We wouldn't want to keep you in on a Saturday morning."

"It's my room as much as yours," Meg retorted, not budging.

The older girls were working on their French homework. Sal glared at Meg but did not waste breath trying to persuade her.

"Listen, Els," she said and she read a sentence aloud.

Meg began to kick the wall rhythmically, thump...thump...thump!

"MEG!" Sal thundered.

"What?" Meg asked, innocently, her eyes gleaming.

"She's not hurting us, Sal," Elsje put in quietly. She smiled a little at Meg. Meg's foot dropped back onto the bed. Why was it that when Elsje's calm gray eyes met yours, you suddenly knew, without any telling, how silly you were being?

It was at that moment the phone sounded.

Meg scrambled off the bed and charged into the hall, bound and bent to be the first one there. She snatched the receiver from the hook, and then had to catch her breath before she said, "Hello."

"Mrs. Andrew Copeland, please. Long distance is calling," the operator singsonged.

"Just a moment, please," Meg said politely. Then, covering the mouthpiece with her hand, she shouted, "MO-THER! LONG DISTANCE!!"

"All right, all right," Mother said, shaking her head at her daughter's bellow. "Tell the others lunch is ready and go on to the table. I'll be there in a minute."

Meg wanted to linger and see who was calling, but Mother waved her away. They were halfway through the first course before Emily Copeland joined them.

"Guess what?" she said breathlessly as she took her place. The family could see, from the excitement on her face, that they would never guess.

"The Martians have landed," Kent tried, halfheartedly.

"Polly is going to be married!" Mother announced.

There was a general outcry.

"Aunt Polly?"

"Married?"

"But she didn't say a word last week..."

"Who's she marrying, Mother?"

"Hush, the whole lot of you, and I'll explain," Mother said. All at once, she remembered Elsje and sent her a special smile.

"You've met my sister Polly, haven't you, Elsje," she said, trying to remember. Her face cleared. "But of course you have. When they were here last summer, Sal stayed at your place."

"Oh, Mother! Elsje knows her. *Go on!*" Sally protested.

"She is marrying Charles Preston," Mother told them, "and the wedding is to be a week from today. We're all invited."

"Mr. Preston? Isn't he the guy that lives next door to Grandma and Aunt Polly?" Kent interrupted.

"But he has three children!" Mindy cried, before Mother could answer. "Susan Preston is as old as I am."

"You're both right," Mother laughed. "And if you'll all stop interrupting, I'll tell you the whole story. The Prestons lived in that same house next to ours when we were children...

28

Andrew, imagine Polly getting married to Charles! After all these years!"

Mother bounced on her chair as though she were younger than Meg, and the others laughed at her.

"You're interrupting your own self," accused Meg.

"I can't help it," Mother said. But she went on with the story.

"When we were in high school, Charles and Polly went everywhere together. They both went to Queens and he took her to all the dances. We just took it for granted that they would marry eventually."

"What happened?" Mindy prompted as Mother paused, looking back over the years.

"Charles went to England for a year of study. He's a history professor, you know. He was given a traveling scholarship. And while he was there, he married an English girl. When we heard, we were so worried about how to tell Polly—and then it turned out that Charles had written to her weeks before and she knew all about it."

"How terrible!" Melinda's eyes were dark with sympathy. Then they grew puzzled. "But I thought Aunt Polly and Mrs. Preston were best friends."

"So they were." Mother laughed at Mindy's startled face. "Polly was the very first one to go over and call on Anna Preston when Charles brought her home. Polly took her a pumpkin pie—and Anna had never tasted pumpkin pie before. The next thing we knew, the two of them were friends. The Prestons had three children...Susan and Jane and...Jock, I think. Anyway, they all call Polly 'Aunt' just as you do."

Meg had stopped eating and was listening with both ears. She had never dreamed an aunt could be so interesting. Mother's face grew grave as she told them of Mrs. Preston's death four years before. Polly Kent had taken in the Preston children while their mother was in the hospital and had done everything she could to help. Charles Preston had hired a housekeeper after his wife's death, but Polly still managed to do the extras. She made party dresses for the girls and went to school concerts and took over special desserts and helped with homework. When Charles Preston was offered a university appointment in British Columbia, he discovered, suddenly, that neither he nor his children could live without Polly. The Prestons were packed, ready to leave, when he proposed.

"And when Polly agreed to go with them, they put off their departure for one week," Mother finished. "It sounds as though Polly will be spending all week at the sewing machine. Jane and Susan are going to be bridesmaids. They're all flying to Vancouver next Saturday."

"Grandma must be having a fit at the thought of flying to Vancouver," Kent laughed. "I've heard her say lots of times she doesn't believe in flying! 'If the Lord had wanted us to fly, He'd have made us with wings,'" he quoted.

"Grandma isn't going with them, Kent," Mother said quietly.

"Isn't going...!" the children echoed. Dad waited, watching Mother.

"She was invited to go but she has refused. It must have been terribly hard for her. She and Polly have been keeping house together, just the two of them, ever since my father died. That's almost twenty years ago. But Grandma says that Polly has other responsibilities now with a whole new family... That was one of Polly's reasons for phoning. Mother says that she will go into a Senior Citizens' Home."

"You don't think that's the answer, do you," Dad asked gently.

"I don't know, Andrew. I really don't know. But I think we'll have to offer. And I'm almost certain she'll come."

"That settles it," Dad said. He grinned at the blank looks on the children's faces. "Grandma will be coming home with us," he explained.

Kent opened his mouth to protest but thought better of it as he saw the look his mother and father were exchanging. His parents had a private language which needed no spoken words.

"I'm sorry. I know it will be hard," Mother was telling him this time. And Dad was telling her it would be all right and he loved her.

Meg had caught the look too but she did not read its meaning. She only knew that it made her feel left out. She wrinkled up her nose and shoved away the fruitcake which Mindy was passing to her.

"I hate that stuff," she declared emphatically. "It has *peel* in it."

"You'd think 'peel' was a bad word to hear you say it," Mindy laughed.

"Watch out the wind doesn't change," Kent warned his younger sister. "Your nose might stay like that forever."

Meg searched for a comeback. Then she hooted, "When did the wind change on you? You've had that awful face ever since I can remember!"

Kent scowled, but Dad laughed with Meg.

"A couple of years of practice, Emily, and we'll have a wit on our hands," he said.

"Yeah! A nitwit!" Kent redeemed himself.

"But where will Grandma sleep?" Melinda asked, not diverted by their teasing. "We don't have another bedroom."

Mother frowned. The children watched her as she moved the furniture around inside her head. Meg was still not alarmed. She knew that Grandma was coming, but Grandma had come before. Someone slept on the couch for a few days until Grandma went home. She had not yet grasped the fact that, this time, Grandma would not be leaving.

"I suppose somebody is going to have to move downstairs to the recreation room," Mother said, after a long moment. "It's too bad because we'll be needing that room more than ever now. It is going to be quite an adjustment for Mother, living with all of us, after years of being in her own house with just Polly at home."

"I'll sleep down there," Kent offered at once.

"He's planning to watch *The Late Show* every night," Melinda guessed, and guessed rightly, but before she had finished speaking, Mother was shaking her head.

"Your room is too small for Grandma and it has no closet," she reminded her son. "I think it will have to be Melinda..."

"But I was going to move in with Mindy!" Sal objected.

"You can't manage those cellar stairs," Mother reminded her. "It's all very well sliding down on your behind when you want to see some special T.V. program...but I think you must all realize that this is going to be a permanent thing. Grandma will still be here with us next September when Mindy leaves for college. You'll only be wanting a place to sleep weekends then, Mindy. I know you two girls were looking forward to sharing a room, but you can see for yourselves that it just wouldn't work out..."

Sal, clearly disappointed, was staring down at her plate. Melinda looked uncomfortable. She had agreed to room with her younger sister when her parents had suggested it. Even she had been aware of the increasing friction between Sally and Meg. Just the same, she had always had a room of her own and, right now, she had a great deal of studying to do. Should she try to explain how little it really mattered to her—and perhaps hurt Sal—or should she leave well enough alone? She was still dithering when Meg, all in a flash, grasped the significance of everything they had been saying in the last few minutes.

She sprang to her feet, sending her chair over backwards with a crash. Her eyes were blazing, her cheeks aflame with indignation and fear.

"You said...YOU PROMISED I COULD HAVE A ROOM OF MY OWN!!" she stormed at Mother. "You PROMISED!"

"That's enough, Meg," Mother said in a quiet voice which had the strength of steel. "It can't be helped. I'm sorry because I know how badly you must feel, but I did not know that your grandmother...Meg, wait!"

But Meg was gone. She flew from the room, from their reasoning and sympathy, from the certain knowledge that, however sorry they sounded, they would still take her room away from her.

Once in the hall, she slowed to a walk. She needed to be by herself—and she could not be alone in the room she and Sal shared. Long ago, she had been forced to find a private place to do her crying. First she had used the broom cupboard, but when she grew bigger she discovered that everyone knew why she went there, so she had discovered a new place and kept it to herself. Without making a sound, even holding her breath so that she would not sob and betray herself, she turned into her parents' room and crawled under the bed.

Then she lay still, face down on the carpet, and, as quietly as she could, she cried her heart out.

4
Grandma Comes

MEG DID NOT TELL Charlotte at first. She still hoped that somehow Mother would manage to keep her word.

"It's not Mother's fault, Meg." Sal tried to reason with her when they were alone in their room on Monday night. "She couldn't know Grandma was coming. Why don't you grow up and think about somebody else's side for a change? Don't forget—I'm stuck with you too. And you're not what I'd call the perfect roommate!"

"Leave me ALONE!" Meg howled at her.

"What's the matter, girls?" Dad called.

They were both silent. Then Sal called back, "Nothing."

The next afternoon, Mother picked Meg up after school. Meg climbed into the car without even saying hello.

"What sort of new dress would you like for

Aunt Polly's wedding, Margaret Ann?" Mother prodded lightly.

"I don't care."

"You know, there's one solution, Meg," Mother said wearily, keeping her eyes on the traffic. "You could have the room in the basement, the one we're fixing up for Melinda. It would be awkward all around, but if it means so much to you, I suppose we could manage it somehow."

It was clear that Mother did not want to offer Meg the recreation room as a bedroom. All her earlier reasons still stood in the way. Those reasons, however, held no reality for Meg. Still, she could not accept. She had reasons of her own for not accepting. First of all, the recreation room was still going to belong to the whole family, whoever slept in it. They were not going to disturb Mindy when she was studying, but whenever she was out or just relaxing, the rest of them were to be free to use the room as they always had. Melinda was really going to camp out in it rather than own it. Meg, on the other hand, wanted a room all her own, a room with a key for the door, a room she would not have to share with anyone at any time.

There was another reason why she could not agree—and Mother knew it as well as Meg did. Meg was afraid of the night. Even though Mother left the hall light on, Meg often saw tigers crouching in dim corners of the room before she went to sleep. If a car threw light on the wall, Meg would stiffen with terror, knowing it to be a burglar's flashlight. She had learned, over the years, to argue with herself when she grew afraid. "Listen," she would tell herself sternly, "you can hear them talking in the kitchen." The sound of Dad's laugh would reassure her. She could not bear to lie awake with a long, dark stairway between herself and everyone else.

"You promised me I could have the room I'm in now," she said stubbornly. Then inspiration struck. "Why can't Grandma sleep down there?"

"Oh, Meg, don't be so silly," Mother said crossly.

I'm not silly! Meg protested hotly, to herself, as they parked the car and walked to the store where children's clothes were sold. Why shouldn't Grandma sleep in the cellar? If it's good enough for Mindy, it's good enough for Grandma! And Mother did promise!

The dress they chose was the loveliest Meg had ever owned. It was dark brown velvet with a full skirt. There was a narrow ruffle of lace around the throat, and there were two tiny puckered pockets in the skirt which were also edged with lace. Meg took a fold of the material between her thumb and finger and felt its deep, mossy richness. Standing before the triple mirror, she almost smiled at the several selves she saw. Just in time, she remembered her anger.

"Well, what about it, honey?" Mother was ignoring her clouded face. "You're the one who'll have to wear it."

Meg stared stonily at her reflection. Mother always let them make the final choice when it came to clothes. For once, Meg wished she would not. Mother was still waiting. The salesgirl looked at Meg inquiringly.

"It's okay, I guess," she mumbled.

"If you don't like it, we can look elsewhere..." Mother began. Then her eyes met Meg's in the mirror. "We'll take it," Mother told the clerk quietly.

Meg let out the breath she had been holding. She forgave Mother everything, in that instant. It was really not Mother's fault anyway. It was Grandma's. Sal had said so.

When the two of them were leaving the store, Meg reached for the dress box.

"I'll carry it," she said gruffly. "I've never had a velvet dress before," she went on.

"You had a blue velvet dress when you were two years old," Mother informed her. "Grandma and Aunt Polly gave it to you."

They drove home in silence.

"You lucky thing!" Charlotte said, when Meg told her the whole story. Meg stared at her, astonished. Charlotte added quickly, "Well, heck, I've never been to a wedding!"

"Oh," Meg said.

Even Charlotte did not understand.

The wedding was a disappointment to Meg. Jane and Susan were dressed as proper bridesmaids. Their dresses were not floor-length, but they were pale yellow taffeta and they had hoops underneath. Aunt Polly was the one who spoiled it. Instead of a white satin wedding gown with a train, she wore a blue party dress. Mother, Melinda and Sally loved it.

"The blue positively sparkles," Mother breathed.

"It's really the cut of it that makes it right," Melinda judged.

Sal said softly, "It just matches her eyes."

But Meg knew better. Aunt Polly simply did not look like a bride!

After the ceremony, the guests crowded into the church parlor. There were chairs for many of the grown-ups but the children had to stand. Dad made a speech and everyone but Meg roared with laughter. There were more toasts. Mr. Preston made a speech too. Sandwiches were passed, and then slices of the tall wedding cake.

Meg was squashed into a corner, hemmed in by people she did not know. She felt as though she were drowning in a sea of adult conversation. Nobody paid any attention to her velvet dress. Jane Preston, flush with excitement, went by. She was still holding her small bouquet and wearing a little cap which looked like a circle of flowers.

"Janie, you look adorable," one of the Preston aunts said, catching her by the arm. "I don't see how Polly managed it in just one week. You look exactly like a primrose!"

Jane blushed pinker than ever and held her bouquet a little higher.

"She wobbled going down the aisle though," Meg said, under her breath, to the beaming aunt.

Unable to bear it another second, Meg looked for someone to rescue her. Aunt Polly had disappeared and Mother with her. Kent had ducked out long ago with Jock Preston and Melinda was deep in a conversation with Susan. Meg knew better than to join them.

"How are you getting along, Margaret?" Grandma was suddenly standing in front of her.

Grandma had a new dress too. She did not have a bouquet but she was wearing a corsage. Meg, who had never seen an orchid before, did not approve of it. It looked spidery. Still, she thought gloomily, it was something extra. Looking at the flower instead of at her grandmother, she answered flatly, "I'm fine, thank you."

She glanced up then in time to see a funny

look on Grandma's face. Almost as though Grandma too were fighting tears.

"Oh, Mrs. Kent," the Preston aunt cried rapturously just then, "what an exquisite wedding! And how lucky our Charles is..."

Meg escaped. She wriggled through the crowd until she reached the hall. Then, still hearing the buzzing talk behind her, she slipped out the side door of the church and stood on the lawn. It was cold out there. She would have to go in almost at once. But she took a deep breath of the fresh biting air and felt suddenly free.

Then she saw her mother and Aunt Polly. They were on their way back along the walk from the minister's house. Now Meg remembered the others talking about Aunt Polly's being invited to change in the manse, since everything at the Kents' house was packed up ready for the movers.

The two women paused in front of the church. Neither of them saw Meg, huddled into the corner of the doorway.

"Oh, Em," Aunt Polly said, "I'm going to miss you so."

"It's not the end of the world," Mother returned—and suddenly Meg knew that they were crying.

She opened the door a crack and slid back into the church. Once inside, she stood very still for a moment, her eyes thoughtful and a little frightened.

The stories Mother had told them of the far-off days when she and Aunt Polly were children together took on a new meaning all at once.

Someday, Mindy will get married, Meg thought confusedly, and—Sal! And everything will change!

Then she sped down the hall, running back to the comfort of the noisy party. As she burst into the room, she collided with her father.

"Stay with me, Meg," he said forlornly. "I feel lost in this mob."

Meg clutched his broad palm gratefully and stuck to him like a burr until it was time to go home.

Grandma came home with them. It was a tight squeeze in the back seat. Meg had to perch on the edge to make room, propping her feet on Sal's crutches. Sal and Mindy went over the entire wedding, with Grandma putting in comments here and there. Meg said nothing at all. Grandma kept worrying about Aunt Polly's being up in an airplane.

"She promised to send us a wire," she said for the third time.

Meg's shoulders twitched with impatience. The trip home was taking centuries. It was dark already outside the car window. The new velvet dress was getting bunched up and the lace collar was scratching her neck.

"Stop for a minute, Andrew," Mother said suddenly. "All right, children, out you get and stretch!"

They objected, but Mother insisted that they all clamber out, even Sal. They stood hunched against the January wind, unable to see each other clearly.

"We're freezing out here, Mother," Melinda complained.

"All right, hop in," Mother ordered. "You sit in front this time, Melinda, and keep the men company."

When the car was back on the highway, Mother reached out and pulled Meg onto her lap. Meg's legs stuck out awkwardly. She was really too big to be sitting on laps. She stayed obstinately erect for a few minutes. Then, in spite of herself, she let Mother draw her back to rest against her shoulder. An unexpected tear slid down the side of her nose. She put out her tongue and licked it off her cheek. Mother did not appear to notice it. She began to sing softly, so softly that Meg could hardly make out the words. Not that it mattered. She knew them by heart. She had had them sung to her since she was a baby.

Golden slumbers kiss your eyes.
Smiles await you when you rise.

Sleep, pretty darling, do not cry,
And I will sing a lullaby.

Sal and Melinda joined in on the second verse, but Meg was asleep and did not hear them.

When they reached home, Meg was still half asleep as she stumbled up the walk and into the house. She was too groggy to feel her usual twinge of envy when Susie ignored her completely and hurled her shaggy self at Sal instead.

"She always thinks I've left home forever," Sal murmured fondly, balancing precariously on one crutch while she stooped to scratch the soft terrier's ears.

"Here's your room, Mother," Mother's voice came from down the hall.

Grandma stopped outside the door.

"But isn't this Melinda's room?" she asked.

She sounded terribly stiff and strange.

"I have a new room, an elegant one, downstairs," Melinda assured her. She carried one of Grandma's bags in and put it on the bed.

"Am I putting anyone else out?" Grandma asked, stiff in that starchy voice.

Meg opened her mouth to tell Grandma all about it when Mother silenced her with a look like a sword thrust. She spoke gently to Grandma, who had missed the look.

"Don't be silly, Mother. Would we have asked

you to come if we hadn't room for you?"

"See, Grandma," Sal said gaily, throwing open their bedroom door. "Meg and I are in here right next to you. We'll see that you behave."

Grandma walked to their door and looked in

Now she'll see, Meg thought exultantly. There's not enough room for two—and I'm the only one without a desk!

Grandma turned to face the cluster of Copelands.

"It's good for youngsters to share a room," she said. She sounded sure of herself, suddenly. She added, "You're a fortunate girl, Margaret, to have a dear girl like Sally for your roommate."

She went into her own room. The rest of the family scattered. Meg stood as though she were rooted to the floor. At last she whispered, "I hate you, Grandma."

Nobody was listening. As usual, nobody was paying any attention to her at all. So she said it once more before she ran away.

"I hate you."

5
From Bad to Worse

HATING GRANDMA was not quite as easy as Meg had thought it would be. She had to seize on little things.

On that first Sunday morning, when the Copelands were on their way into church, Meg realized, halfway up the aisle, that Grandma was the person behind her. They reached the place where they usually sat. Meg, wanting to sit beside her mother, who would have a pad of paper and a pencil stub in her pocket to keep Meg from squirming during the sermon, hung back so that Grandma would go in ahead of her. Dad, standing aside to allow his family to enter the pew, looked down at his youngest in surprise. Another family was trying to pass and Meg was in the way. Grandma reached back, took her by the elbow, and piloted her into the pew. Meg could not balk before the whole congregation, but she fumed inside.

Before she had calmed down, it was time for the first hymn. Since she had been very small, Meg had had a habit of swaying from side to side while she sang. Mother had told her about it often and she tried to remember, but this morning she was busy thinking about Grandma "pushing" her like that.

"Stand still, child," Grandma hissed at her.

Meg, catching herself rocking, stopped too quickly and nearly lost her balance. She clutched at the pew in front for support, and her hymnbook slipped from her hand and crashed to the floor. Dad looked at her severely. Everyone in the family caught that look.

"Come to my heart, oh thou wonderful love," the congregation sang.

But Meg was not listening.

"Bossy old thing," she raged under her breath.

When they came out of church, she was not speaking to anybody. But not one of her family appeared to notice her angry silence. They all started arguing about hymn tunes. Melinda was tired of the old ones sung over and over again. Sal maintained that they did not sing enough familiar ones. Dad stuck up for Sal and Mother took Mindy's side. Grandma said that the best old hymns, like "Dare to Be a Daniel," were not even in the new hymnal. Kent was astonished that Grandma could call the hymnal "new."

"We've had those exact same ones in the church ever since I was born!" he protested.

"I've never even heard 'Dare to Be a Daniel,'" Sal supported him.

The three grown-ups were shocked. "Of course you have," they chorused.

Sal shook her head stubbornly. Kent and Mindy seconded her. Meg remained silent. Now they would notice. But instead, they began to sing.

Many mighty men are lost,
Daring not to stand,
Who for God had been a host
By joining Daniel's band.

Dare to be a Daniel.
Dare to stand alone.
Dare to have a purpose firm.
Dare to make it known.

On the second chorus, the three older children joined in. Meg held out until the third. Then the brave swing of the old tune pulled her into it with the rest of them.

After dinner, Meg changed into her old clothes. She had the room to herself. Sal had taken Susie and gone over to Libby's for the afternoon. Meg leaned over to tie her shoes. She jerked on her left lace to tighten it and the frayed string came apart in her hands. Meg grunted and straightened up. It was useless for her to try to fasten it together. Meg's knots were hopeless affairs which slipped undone the moment she thought them secure. She went to find her mother.

In the hall outside her bedroom door, she paused, suddenly aware of the strange stillness in the house. Meg could remember Sunday afternoons when the Copeland family had done special things together. They had gone walking in the woods or had sat and popped corn over the fire while Dad read aloud. But now, everybody but Meg had outgrown family excursions. Kent had gone to the river with Mike Jackson to play hockey on the bumpy wind-rippled ice. Melinda was down in her room, reading *Jane Eyre* for the ninth time. She had hung on the cellar door a huge sign which warned TRESPASSERS WILL BE BEHEADED. Grandma was lying down. Dad had gone to a meeting at the church. Mother...where was Mother?

"Mother! Where are you?"

"Right here." Mother's voice sounded reassuringly alive and close by. Meg followed it to the kitchen. Her mother was standing by the counter next to the sink, arranging flowers. They were pink and white carnations, and Mother was coaxing them into place in the blue boat-shaped bowl. She always handled flowers as though she expected them to sense her caring and to respond to it with their utmost beauty.

"Look." Meg stood at her elbow and displayed one-third of a grimy shoelace. "It needs fixing."

"It needs to be thrown out," Mother said, wrinkling her nose at the raveling, limp end of lace. "I'll get you some new ones. Meg, I wish you'd clean those shoes. They're disgraceful."

Meg looked down at her old gym shoes.

"But they're just my old shoes. They're supposed to be like that."

Mother sighed and went to fetch new laces. Meg pulled out one of the kitchen chairs and sat down to wait. Absently, she began to pile up the various things which people had left lying around on the table—first the big yellow mixing bowl, then Mindy's Latin book, then the plastic container full of leftover gravy, then the church calendar...

"Meg!" Mother exclaimed.

Meg jumped and her hand knocked into the unsteady stack of objects. The bowl glided smoothly out from underneath and landed on the floor. The plastic container overturned. Gravy flowed in a thick brown river across the front of Mindy's book. Mother caught the church calendar out of harm's way and glared at her daughter.

Meg looked down at the bowl. "It didn't

break," she announced hopefully.

Mother groaned and tore her hair with her free hand. But Meg could see that she was saved by the laughter in her mother's eyes.

"Epaminondas, I do declare, you ain't got the sense you was born with," Mother complained in mock woe.

Meg giggled and got down to pick up the bowl. Thank goodness it had not smashed. Mother took the Latin book over to the sink.

"Tell me the story of Epaminondas," Meg begged.

"You get busy with those shoelaces...and tell me what you want for your birthday," Mother replied, scraping gravy off a picture of Julius Caesar.

Meg scowled. She had thought and thought. It seemed to her that this year they owed her something special. They had promised her her own room. She knew now that she was not going to be given that. Well then, she meant to ask for something just as important, just as wonderful. If they loved her, they would get it for her. If they did not, she would at least know for certain. The only trouble was that she had not yet been able to conjure up something special enough to ask for.

"I can't decide," she told her mother.

"I've never known you not to have a list a yard long," Mother said, turning to look at her with searching eyes.

Meg ducked her head down to escape them. She finished lacing her shoes and tied them, after a fashion. "Mother..." she began then.

"I know exactly what you're going to say," Mother told her. She set the Latin book on edge to dry and went back to the carnations.

"What?" Meg challenged.

"Mother, there's nothing to do around here." Mother imitated Meg's voice perfectly. "Mother, what'll I do?"

The words came so close to those she had been about to utter that Meg's mouth made an O of surprise. Then she rallied.

"I was not going to say any such thing," she denied too hotly. "I was going to say...let's go for a walk."

"Honey, look outside. It's snowing hard."

"I like walking in snow...and there's nobody around here to do anything with. We used to go walking when it snowed. I remember once when we went away out to where the river forks."

"I remember that day," Mother said. "It was lovely. We sang 'Walking in a Winter Wonderland.' We took Sal on a sled."

"Well, why can't we go today?" Meg put in.

Mother carried the bowl of flowers into the dining room. She came back and gave Meg a quick hug. Meg, who was feeling as bunched up and prickly as a porcupine, did not hug her back.

"Even if it weren't so cold, Grandma is resting and I don't want to disturb her. I wouldn't want her to wake up on her first day here and find we'd all deserted her."

Grandma! She might have known that somehow it would be Grandma's fault.

"Why don't you get a good book?" Mother suggested.

"I hate good books," Meg flung back as she went banging back to her room.

"Be quiet, Meg," Mother's voice came after her. "I told you Grandma was resting!"

Meg lay on her stomach on the bed. It was a dark afternoon but she did not put on a light. After a few moments, she noticed Sally's pen lying on the windowsill. She reached for it idly. Then she uncapped it and began to draw on the back of her hand. She made a big bell with a flourishing bow at the top. She held it away from her for a second, admiring it. Then she lettered carefully on the side of the bell *Grandma is my enemy*.

6
Enemies Shouldn't
Be Friendly

"DID THE OLD witch come?" Charlotte asked cheerfully on Monday morning.

"She's not an old witch." Meg defended Grandma. Meg might not like her grandmother, but Grandma was still one of her family and Meg was loyal.

Charlotte laughed. "Mine sure is," she said ruefully.

Meg knew Charlotte's grandmother and she did not argue. Mrs. Medford was like a witch. Her black eyes bored holes in you and her queer cracked laugh was like a cackle. Mrs. Russell sent Charlotte regularly to call on her, but even breezy, self-confident Charlotte was frightened by Mrs. Medford.

That morning, for the first time, Meg sat at her desk and wasted time on purpose.

She had never been good at keeping her mind

on her work. She wrote slowly, gripping her pencil so tightly her knuckles whitened, and after a few minutes her whole hand ached. But until that Monday morning, she had always flushed guiltily when Miss Armstrong caught her resting and said, "Get busy, Meg!" or "Meg, you're behind again." Always, she had struggled, briefly, to catch up, tried to make her fingers race like Charlotte's, resolved to keep her thoughts where they belonged, planned to finish first this time and surprise everyone.

It had never worked. Meg's fingers did not know how to race. In no time at all, her thoughts escaped her and rambled off on their own. The allotted half hour would be up and she would have hardly begun and Miss Armstrong would sigh again. "Don't you care?" the teacher would ask. Meg had always cared, more than Miss Armstrong imagined, more than her family believed, far more than even Charlotte guessed.

But she had decided not to care any longer. Mother had broken her promise. Meg was not going to keep hers.

But it was not easy. For the first time, Meg was aware of the tick of the classroom clock. She fiddled with her eraser. She shifted in her seat. Like a puppy who has wandered away from home, Meg was not really enjoying her new freedom.

"Meg, hurry up," Miss Armstrong said.

Meg's cheeks reddened, but although she took up her pencil and bent over her book, she did not hurry.

She was kept in every night that week.

Grandma said nothing about it at first. All during those early days, Grandma behaved carefully.

"You'd think she was somebody we hardly knew," Sal wondered.

It was Tuesday night. The three girls were doing the supper dishes. Mindy was washing; Sal, perched on a stool, was drying; and Meg was supposed to be putting away. The tray was full. Sal was beginning to wedge things into places too small for them. Meg, who should have carried the tray into the dining room, loitered to listen.

"She acts like a guest," Mindy agreed. They had lowered their voices. "You know how it is when you're visiting... You don't want to get up too early and waken people but you don't want to be the last one down to breakfast and keep them waiting. I hate that part of being a guest."

Meg hated it too. Once she had gone to stay overnight with a girl named Nancy Miller. Nancy's mother did not approve of children's sleeping together "talking half the night," so Meg had been put in a big spare bed, all by herself. She still remembered lying there in the morning, straining her ears for any sound of movement in the rest of the house.

"I'll bet she misses Aunt Polly too," Sal said. "Look at the way she keeps waiting for letters although its only been three days since they left. Meg, for goodness' sake, take these things before something breaks!"

"I *am!*" Meg retorted.

She had waited too long. The tray was overloaded. One of the glasses began to topple. Meg put the tray down again hastily.

"Really!" Mindy said, like a grown-up. She dried her hands and came to help.

As each day passed, Grandma became a little more relaxed. On Wednesday, she walked to the library with Sal. Although Susie was a well-trained dog, it was still easier for Sal if somebody else held the leash. Managing her canes on the snowy sidewalk was challenge enough. Grandma carried books and held the leash. Sal, who liked to act as though she did not need help, made a point of telling Grandma how grateful she was.

Meg, arriving home from school, met them at the end of the walk. The four of them walked into the house together. Just inside the door, they paused to brush snow off one another.

"Where have you been?" Grandma said pleasantly.

"Nowhere." Meg bent down to pull off her

boots.

"She's just come home from school," Sal explained somewhere over her head.

"Oh," Grandma said. It was half a question, but when neither of the girls supplied any more information, Grandma busied herself drying Susie off and undoing her leash.

On Thursday, Mother asked Grandma at breakfast how she managed to keep cabbage rolls from drying out. Grandma spent the rest of the morning in the kitchen and everyone enjoyed the result at suppertime. Kent smacked his lips audibly, Dad rubbed his full stomach and groaned.

"I haven't cooked for two men in a long time," Grandma said, her voice pleased.

When they sat down to supper on Friday evening, Grandma was no longer a guest. She did not even bother to take off her apron. She did not hesitate to ask questions.

"Margaret, the older ones all get home from school long before you do almost every afternoon. What keeps you late so often?" she wanted to know.

Meg took a big mouthful of scrambled eggs. It was not polite to talk with your mouth full.

Kent was happy to explain. "She stays in with Miss Armstrong, Grandma. Miss Armstrong would drop dead of shock if Meg and Charlotte left at four with the rest of the class."

"But not every night..." Grandma began, sure he was teasing.

"This week, next week, sometime...ever," Kent quoted flippantly.

"But...why?" Grandma was troubled. She appealed now to Meg's parents.

"I really don't understand it myself, Mother," Emily Copeland answered. She sounded tired all at once. Kent concentrated on his eggs and wished he had kept quiet.

"Meg's just a slow starter. She's going to dazzle us all yet," Dad said lightly. "Would you please pass the chili sauce, Mindy?"

Melinda passed the chili sauce. Nobody said anything. Meg picked up her glass and took a long drink of milk, but the clink of the glass on the tabletop only made the silence louder.

"Are you going to be in this evening, Emily?" Grandma's words cracked through the unnatural hush too abruptly, but the Copelands picked up the topic of conversation gratefully. There was talk of the meeting Mother was going to. The United Church Women were showing a film on India. Mother had to be there early to prepare refreshments.

Yet, although Meg was relieved to have the silence ended and the subject changed, she reminded herself that Grandma had been the one who brought up the subject and made the silence in the beginning. Grandma had been the one to bring the worry into Mother's eyes, and so had forced Meg to remember the week's work she had let slide by, mostly undone.

She went on to list to herself other grievances she had collected against Grandma. Grandma had dusted in their room yesterday and had broken Meg's statue of a small, knock-kneed fawn. One day at lunch, Grandma had pointed out that Meg's hands were dirty when nobody else would have noticed. Grandma had tripped over Meg's skates, left lying in the middle of the hall, and she had complained to Mother that she might have broken her neck—although she had caught at the door frame and had not even fallen down really. Grandma shuddered every time Meg let a door slam accidentally. On Wednesday night, after supper, when Meg had thought to slip out for a minute and see Charlotte, Grandma had asked her where she was going. Of course, she had asked loudly enough so that Dad had heard and lectured Meg. Meg was not allowed out after supper on a school night.

"She really is my enemy," Meg decided darkly. "She likes all the others. It's just me she picks on. She never calls Sally 'Sarah.'"

But Grandma came to the bedroom door when Meg was putting on her pajamas.

"Would you like me to read to you?" she asked.

When Meg did not answer at once, her grandmother filled in the pause nervously. "I know your mother reads to you usually...but she couldn't have had time tonight... If you'd rather wait though..."

"We're reading *Anne of Ingleside*," Meg interrupted. She heard the stand-offishness in her own voice but she could not help it. Grandma was to blame. She was acting like a guest again, hesitating in the doorway, twisting her ring around and around on her finger.

"If you'd rather wait..." Grandma repeated helplessly.

"No," Meg said quickly, turning her back and taking a running leap into bed. "The book's there on the dresser. Mother left the place marked."

The moment Grandma began, Meg realized that she had forgotten the way her grandmother read. Mother skimmed through the story. Sometimes her tongue tripped over the words which came tumbling out of her mouth. When the book grew particularly exciting, Mother sometimes could not resist skipping. Meg did not want her mother to change her manner of reading. It was fun to fly through books with Mother. But Grandma read properly. Grandma took time for every word. Grandma somehow became Anne and Gilbert and Walter and Susan Baker and Aunt Mary Maria, each in turn. It was like being at a play. Meg forgot all about being enemies as she listened. She forgot Grandma entirely and lived, for a moment, in a house on Prince Edward Island.

And Grandma did not stop at the end of the chapter. When Sal came into the room at nine-thirty, both Meg and Mrs. Kent had lost track of time. Walter Blythe had just walked all the way home from Lowbridge in the middle of the night because he had been told that his mother was dying. And Ingleside was dark!

"What's got into you two?" Sally demanded. "Meg was supposed to be asleep half an hour ago."

Meg, who was weeping over Walter, still had the presence of mind to glare, through her tears, at her sister. But before she could bite Sal's head off, Grandma spoke with unexpected firmness.

"You hush," she said. "If you want to listen, sit down. If you want to chatter, go somewhere else."

Sal laughed and curled up on her bed to hear the end. She remembered this part. When she had been Meg's age, Mother had read this aloud to the three older children—but Mother had stopped at the end of the chapter. Sal had lain awake in an agony of anxiety about Anne. Finally, she had not been able to bear it. She had wriggled down to the foot of the bed and used one of her crutches to pull the book within reach. Mother had put it down nearby when she helped Sal out of her braces. For the first and only time in her life, Sal had sat in the moonlight and read ahead of the others. The next night, when Mother had read aloud how happily it all ended, Sal had not confessed. She had never confessed to this day.

Grandma read straight on to the finish of the tenth chapter. Then she closed the book slowly.

"My, that's a good story," she said, as she rose to go.

She kissed both girls goodnight. Meg kissed her back but she did not say anything.

"You could have thanked her," Sal scolded after Grandma had disappeared.

"She liked doing it," Meg said, her mouth setting mulishly.

She turned over then, away from Sally, so that the uneasiness inside her would not show. Grandma had liked doing it. But she, Meg, had liked having Grandma do it too. She had been so certain that Grandma was against her, so sure they were doomed to be enemies. And yet, Grandma had read three whole chapters.

"Enemies shouldn't be friendly," Meg protested.

She could still have been arguing with Sal. But Sal had departed to brush her teeth. Meg pulled the covers right over her head. She curled up small in her hidden nest. They were all shut out now. She was safe in here.

"Go to sleep," she ordered the part of herself which was still asking questions. "Just go to sleep."

7
Sparks Fly

MOTHER SUGGESTED a birthday sleigh ride. "Make a list," she told Meg. "Mr. Benton told me that the sleigh would hold twelve to fifteen people."

Meg was writing the tenth name when Mother happened to glance over her shoulder. "Oh, honey, not that many!" she objected.

"You said fifteen."

"How about us?" Mother said. "There are seven of us right here in your family."

Meg blushed. She should have remembered. Of course, she wanted the family to come. But Mother had made a mistake. There were only six...

"Mother, not Grandma?"

Mother looked puzzled and then disturbed. "Don't be silly, Meg. Why shouldn't Grandma go?"

"On a *sleigh ride*?"

Mother tried to remain patient. Her voice sounded thin. "Your grandmother was going on sleigh rides before either you or I were born, silly. She was here when I first thought of it and she said then how long it had been since she had heard the jingle of sleigh bells. You know, Meg, you should ask her sometime to tell you some of the things she used to do when she was your age. You'd be fascinated."

"I'll bet," Meg muttered.

"What did you say?" Mother asked slowly. Her voice sounded dangerous now.

"Nothing." Before Mother could pin her down, Meg added hurriedly, "How will I choose who to ask?"

"Whom," Mother corrected her. She hesitated—as though she were wondering whether the time had come to try to talk things out with Meg once more. Then she sighed and turned away. "That's something you'll have to decide for yourself," she advised brusquely. "Maybe it would be easier to make a new list."

Meg took a blank piece of paper and looked at it. Charlotte was at the top of the other list. But what would Charlotte say when she met Grandma and heard Meg being called Margaret in Grandma's "prunes and prisms" voice. If eight children were to hear it, there was no chance that Meg could escape being called Margaret at school. Abigail Hunter had tried to tell the class her name was Gail, but someone had learned the truth and she had been called Abigail ever since. Even her best friend called her Abbie now. Charlotte would probably end up calling her Maggie.

Meg shuddered.

It was no use appealing to the family. Meg had told them about Abigail and Mother had insisted that Abigail was a lovely name. Mother had a weakness for old-fashioned names. Mother had done the naming in the Copeland family and Dad had invented the nicknames. Mother had chosen the old family names. Melinda Edgeware was a great-great-grandmother or something. Sal was really Sarah Jane like Dad's mother, and Meg was Margaret Ann—just like Grandma. Kent was Mother's maiden name.

None of the others minded. Nothing was known of the first Melinda except her name. The first Sarah Jane Copeland had died before Meg was old enough to remember her. Sal remembered her lovingly—a little brown wren of a woman who lived on a farm and had taken Sal to the barn once to search for eggs. Both grandfathers had died before any of the Copeland children had been born. Kent liked being called Kent. There was no way anyone could turn it into something different.

Nobody else called Meg Margaret. Nobody but Grandma.

"Nobody should shorten a beautiful old name in that ridiculous fashion," Grandma had said once, long before, when Meg had asked why.

Meg had gone to Mother.

"After all, darling, your name *is* Margaret," Mother had answered reasonably. "I often call you Margaret Ann myself. Why hurt Grandma over such a little thing?"

Meg had decided then that it was not worth making a fuss about. After all, Grandma only came for short visits. Over the years, Meg had grown almost used to it. She knew she could never explain the world of difference that lay between the way Grandma said "Margaret" so properly and Mother said "Margaret Ann" so lovingly, turning it into a special name for special moments.

It was only recently that she had begun to wonder why Grandma did not call Sal Sarah—and Mother explained that too, or tried to.

"Sarah was Grandma Copeland's name, and so Mother feels that if your father would rather call his daughter Sal or Sally, she should do the same. It's hard to make it clear, Meg, but Grandma likes to please your father... Do you understand?"

Meg nodded, but privately she thought it a poor excuse. No excuse would do when Charlotte and Marilyn and Bruce and the rest heard Grandma saying...

"Margaret..."

For one startled instant, Meg felt as though her thoughts had risen and spoken aloud. Then she saw Grandma standing before her, frowning at the scratch pad, now covered with doodles, and at the pencil, which by this time was thoroughly chewed.

"...whatever you are supposed to be doing, for goodness' sake, *do* it!" Grandma finished.

Meg simply sat and looked owlishly at her. She had not yet gathered her scattered wits.

"I've never seen such a child for wasting time," Grandma went on, when nobody else said anything. "If you were mine, I'd see to it that..."

"But I'm not yours!"

The words burst out of Meg. They were there in the room before she had thought them to herself. As she stopped to take a breath, Meg could feel them jarring in her ears, as though something had ripped with a harsh, unexpected sound, as though a policeman had shrilled his whistle close to her. If she had looked at her mother just then, Meg might have caught the gleam of sympathy in Mother's eyes. She might have paused for the instant needed to weigh her next words. But Meg did not look at her mother. She was looking at Grandma and seeing her not standing there in the kitchen but sitting in the sleigh. She was hearing

Grandma's voice, clear in the night air, saying "Margaret" and "If you were mine..."

Meg sprang to her feet, instinct warning her that in a minute she would be wanting to run. She dropped, almost threw, her pencil down on the table. It slithered across the polished table top and struck against Grandma's wrist.

"Well, really!" Grandma began, rubbing the spot.

But Meg drowned her out. Meg was past caring. Her first words had crashed open a gate and others plunged through after them.

"I'm not yours. I'm not Margaret. I'm Meg. And I don't want to go on a sleigh ride anyway. Sleigh rides are old-fashioned. Mother told me to make a list of kids to ask but how could I when I hate sleigh rides! Nobody I know would want to go on one..."

Her mind finished the sentence "...when you'd be there ruining everything." Her mouth was open to speak, but at last something stopped her. Grandma—not the one in her mind, but the actual Grandma who stood facing her—looked...stunned.

Once, when Meg was three or four, Mother had asked her what she was doing. "None of your beeswax," Meg had said gaily, lightly, meaning to make a joke, imitating the older ones. And Mother had slapped her. That was the way Grandma looked—as though Meg had slapped her and she did not understand why.

"I'm sorry," Meg gulped, surprising herself almost as much as she had surprised Grandma. Then she fled.

This time, safe in her hiding place, she did not cry. She lay very still for a long time, trying to sort out the muddle she had gotten herself into. It was so tangled. There were so many ifs and buts...

If Mother had kept her promise... If only Grandma had never come... But Grandma had read three chapters... Why did Grandma have to call her Margaret?... If Mother really loved her...but, of course, Mother did...

Finally Meg gave up trying to straighten out the snarls, but she did not come out from under the bed. She began tracing with her index finger the design on the carpet. It was dim in there, like a twilit tent, but Meg knew the pattern of birds and flowers by heart. She went carefully around each pointed petal, curling stem and sharp leaf. She lay lapped in peace, out of harm's reach. She drifted off into a dream.

Then Mother and Sal came into the bedroom. Mother was putting things away in the closet. Meg heard the rustle of plastic. She lay, scarcely breathing, until she realized that they had no idea she was within earshot. They were talking about her. Mother must have already told

Sal about the scene with Grandma.

"But I had troubles when I was her age too," Sal was pointing out. "Don't worry, Mother. Look what a fine, intelligent, well-balanced girl I turned into!"

Meg gritted her teeth. Sally sounded so know-it-all. Next thing, she'd be saying, "It's a phase children go through."

"Come now. You're not quite that grown-up," Mother laughed.

Meg was comforted. Mother was on her side after all. But the next instant, Mother's voice had grown grave again.

"You had troubles, but they weren't the same as Meg's. You were afraid of the whole world, but I understood you. Meg bewilders me. She's hardly spoken to Mother all week, and then out of the blue she explodes. Surely she can't blame Mother for Polly's marriage?... Older people can be a problem, but Mother's been trying so hard not to interfere... And Meg's marks! They're atrocious! Yet the teachers tell me she's bright enough..."

Mother did not usually talk about one child to another in such a fashion. Sal was proud that Mother was sharing her anxieties with her, but at the same time she knew that it was only because Emily Copeland was at her wit's end. Sal wanted to help, but she did not know how. She too had trouble understanding her smaller sister. It was disturbing to find that Mother did not know the answers.

"Maybe she needs a dog," Sal joked, trying to lighten her mother's mood. "You should get her one for her birthday. Not a Westie, mind you! I don't want another West Highland terrier here making my Susie jealous."

"A dog! Do you realize that this house was built to hold five people? And it is now holding seven people and one canine! I'm afraid, if Meg has her heart set on a dog, she's going to have another disappointment coming her way," Mother declared.

Susie, who was never far from Sal, now discovered Meg's presence. She poked her black nose under the edge of the bedspread and sniffed. Meg lay perfectly still and made frightful faces at her.

"Hey, Susie, come out from under there! She's probably looking for your slippers," Sal told her mother. "Susie, come."

Susie backed out.

"I don't understand why she has started chewing things at her age," Sal worried. "Maybe she's trying to get attention. That's what Elsje says. Elsje says some dogs do it when they get bored or lonely. But I can't stay home from school just to keep her company. Maybe we really do need another dog, Mother— to play with Susie."

As they left the room, they were both laughing. Susie padded after them.

Meg drew a deep breath. Her eyes gleamed in the darkness. A dog! That was what she would ask for! Sal had a dog. Mindy had had a cat. Kent had had guinea pigs once. Now he was too busy becoming the world's greatest athlete to have time for a pet. She, Meg, would demand a dog of her own. What's more, she would ask for a Westie, exactly like Susie. That would show them.

"If you won't let me have my own room, you can at least let me have a dog of my own," she practiced as she crawled out from under the bed.

8
What Meg Wanted

MEG ALMOST RUSHED after her mother and announced, then and there, "I know what I want for my birthday—a Westie just like Susie!"

But as she paused inside the bedroom to yank up her tights which were wrinkling around her knees, she realized that if she spoke immediately, Mother would guess at once that she had been listening. And when Mother remembered Susie sniffing under the bed, Meg's private place would be a secret no longer.

I wonder if she already knows, Meg thought, peering cautiously up and down the hall before she stepped out into it. She had been very careful, and she could not think of any time when her mother might have seen a tag-end of her skirt sticking out. But still, it was queer that whenever she flared out at someone and then rushed away in tears, nobody ever followed her.

Were they leaving her alone because Mother made them? Mother was the kind of person who understood when you needed time by yourself. Or was it just that nobody cared enough about her to be curious?

"Come to supper now, Meg," Sal said.

Meg jumped. She knew her cheek was still flushed where it had been pressed on the carpet. Strictly speaking, she had not cried—but there had been moments when she had had to hold her eyes very wide open and concentrate on not letting tears spill over. Facing Sally, Meg felt as though those unshed tears must have marked her cheeks and reddened her eyes.

"I'll be there in a minute," she told her older sister haughtily.

She would go to the bathroom first and splash cold water on her tattletale face. She would comb her rumpled hair.

Sal gave a sudden warm grin and reached out to poke Meg gently with her crutch tip.

"Get a wiggle on, Tagalong Maggie," she said.

Meg began to blush.

"Stop it," she snapped over her shoulder.

But she skipped on her way to the bathroom.

"Tomorrow," she told the Meg in the mirror, "tomorrow I'll ask for a dog."

As she waited for the rest of the day to pass, she began to believe in that dog. Not that they'd give it to her, she reminded herself at first. And she heard again Mother's words—"...if Meg has her heart set on a dog, she's going to have another disappointment coming her way." But pretending never hurt anyone. She was not setting her heart on a make-believe dog. Still, she pictured a small white terrier sleeping at the foot of her bed with his nose tucked between his paws. She pretended the small dog followed her wherever she went. When she came in from school, he scrambled to meet her at the door, falling over his own paws in his hurry to lick her hand. She dreamed of sitting with him, just the two of them together. She would speak his name in a certain soft voice and he would thump his tail joyfully and poke his nose against her, asking for more loving. When she had to scold him, she knew exactly how his ears would go down and his whole shaggy self would look sorry. And he would rest his chin on her foot when she was reading. Susie often did that with Sal. She, Meg, would be every bit as special to her dog as Sal was to Susie.

She dawdled over her dessert.

"Meg, we're all waiting for you," Mindy complained. Mindy was going to a tobogganing party with the Young People's Group. There was still an hour and a half before she had to go, but she pushed up her sleeve and examined her watch anxiously.

"All right, all right," Meg grumbled, shoving

in such enormous bites that Mindy shuddered noticeably.

"Mo-ther! Make her behave!" she cried.

But it was Sal who answered—and she was on Meg's side.

"You wanted her to hurry so she's hurrying. If you don't like it, don't watch," she said tartly. "The party doesn't start till eight anyway."

Meg scooped up the last spoonful, jammed it in and flashed Sal a startled glance. Sal was picking up her crutches and missed it.

When Meg was ready for bed, she suddenly wondered who would read to her tonight. Mother was going out again, Meg knew. She and Dad were the adult advisers for the Young People's Group and they were going along to the toboggan party.

Meg sat on the edge of her bed and wondered what to do next. Her parents were still in the house, but she knew they were almost ready to leave. Grandma had been quiet throughout supper. Thinking back, Meg could not remember that Grandma had said a word. She herself had been so busy thinking about her dog that not until this moment had she been struck by Grandma's silence. Now it sounded as though the family had gathered in the kitchen. Laughter came spilling, teasing and happy, to the place where Meg sat alone. Maybe she should just go to the kitchen door, in her pajamas, and ask the room at large, "Is any-body going to read to me?"

She could read a chapter to herself, of course, but the Copelands did not do that, not with a special bedtime book. She crawled under the covers and lay still instead. She heard more laughter. She heard her father claim that he could toboggan as well as any squirt of a teen-ager. She heard Mindy wail, "Oh, Dad!" The front door slammed. The house was very quiet.

"Did you think I was never coming?" Grandma asked.

Meg stared at her over the edge of the bed-clothes. Grandma did not look at her directly. She fetched the book, switched on the reading lamp, and began—as though Meg had never shouted at her, as though she were just picking up where she had left off. Yet from where she lay, Meg could see the book trembling slightly against the light. And Grandma had to clear her throat twice before she started.

Grandma read two chapters. The suspense was over now. Anne was growing strong and well. But Grandma made a wonderful Rebecca Dew and an even better Miss Cornelia. Meg squirmed with delight as she heard them talk-ing over the terrible Aunt Mary Maria who had descended on the Blythe home for a visit and had, long since, outstayed her welcome.

When Grandma finished, she seemed to take a long time marking the place in the book. Putting it on top of the dresser, she switched off Sally's lamp.

She doesn't know what to do either, Meg thought suddenly, as Grandma felt her way through the darkened room to Meg's bed. In that instant, when she was waiting for her grandmother to kiss her lightly on the cheek, Meg remembered Aunt Mary Maria. Grandma was nothing like her, nothing at all. Meg reared up and flung her arms around her grandmother's neck. She kissed Grandma smack on the mouth, and into that kiss she tried to put all the things she could not explain, all the things she did not understand yet herself.

"Darling, you're strangling me," Grandma gasped.

She steadied herself with one hand on the bed and set her glasses straight on her nose with the other. There was a long moment of silence. Then Grandma cleared her throat again.

"Thank you, Margaret," she said—and she went out of the room.

Meg, who usually simply rolled over, closed her eyes and slept, twisted and turned that night. She did not want to think about Grandma. She began planning her sleigh ride, and then remembered that there was not going to be a sleigh ride. Meg being Meg, she did not once consider trying to take back what she had said.

After a while, she began to wish that Sal would come to bed. The room, which she had so longed to have to herself, seemed empty and full of disturbing shadows. She shut her eyes against them—and there was her little white dog.

She smiled, tucked her hand under her cheek, and settled down to think about him. She would give him a proper name. Nothing silly like Susie. If they were West Highland terriers, they should have Scottish names. Ian... Jock... Angus... Jamie... None of them sounded right. Under her breath, she tried them out. "Here, Jock. Angus, sit." No. There must be other Scottish names. She puzzled over it. Just when she was ready to give up, she remembered her father reading aloud Scottish poems. Robbie Burns. Robbie. That was what she would call him.

"Robbie, come," she said, right out loud. It sounded fine.

She stopped short then. Why, she was really beginning to believe that they would give her this pup called Robbie! They wouldn't. Mother had made no bones about it when she and Sal were talking. She, Meg, had imagined that she wanted them to say no. They would refuse to grant her wish and that would prove that they did not care about her. But she did not want to prove it any longer. She wanted Robbie. He had turned into a real little dog in her mind—just as this room had really been hers before Grandma came. Why, she had done exactly what Mother had said she should not do. She had set her heart on him.

Meg slept badly. She dreamed that Sally was getting married and she, Meg, was hiding in the cellar, crying so hard that she melted the big bouquet she was carrying. Then, suddenly, Charlotte was there, all ready to go on a sleigh ride. "There's not going to be one," Meg cried over and over—but Charlotte did not seem to hear. Then a sleigh pulled up to the door. "See," Charlotte yelled and she pulled Meg out to it. But on every seat, there sat a grandma reading a book. Meg stood there shivering, and then all the grandmas said all at once, "Go and pick up your coat!"

Meg wakened with a start. It was late. Even Mother was in bed, because the hall light was off. The shadows were much deeper now, black as ink, crowding out from every corner. Looking over the edge of her bed, Meg saw something, darker than dark, which seemed to be crawling, inch by inch, along the floor towards her. Outside the window, something creaked sharply.

"Sal!" Meg whispered.

But Sal and Susie were sleeping soundly. They did not stir. Meg lay absolutely still, so still that she ached from holding every finger and toe rigid. She was sure that the thing on the floor was closer now.

It was more than she could bear. She counted to ten, gabbling the numbers. Then she leaped out of bed, shot across the room, reached the door in safety, scurried down the hall and around the corner to her parents' bedroom.

The minute Meg reached the doorway, Mother was awake. She always came instantly wide awake like that when they especially needed her. She threw back the covers and made room for her small shivering daughter.

"What's the trouble, honey?" she whispered.

Meg could not whisper. The explanation poured out of her. It was a muddled-up story of bits and pieces—how badly she wanted a dog of her own, really wanted him—and his name was Robbie—how Sal had been getting married in her dream, how frightened she had been because she had seen something moving on the floor...only she knew it wasn't really—how Sal and Susie and everybody else had had pets and all she had ever had was a turtle, how she wished Grandma would call her Meg, how Grandma picked on her and so did Miss Armstrong and so did Sal and Mindy and Kent, how Robbie was a truly Scottish name...

Long before she had finished, Dad was awake and listening too.

"Please, Mother, please, Daddy," Meg pleaded, her voice hoarse because she was close to crying, "please let me have Robbie for my birthday. I was going to say I wanted him just to get back at Sal but it isn't that. I have to have him. I just have to."

"Cuddle down now and hush," Mother said gently. She pulled the covers right up under Meg's chin, and when Meg opened her mouth to begin all over again, Mother put her hand over it.

"Close your eyes," she ordered. "We'll manage something."

Meg closed her eyes. Now Mother was singing a little of the old lullaby which she had sung in the car a week before. Warmed and beginning to be comforted, Meg slowly stopped shaking. Her breath came more evenly. No shadows reached out for her here. Motller had promised that they would manage. Mother had promised...

When her mother and father began to talk in low voices, she knew she should make herself understand what they were saying. It was important. It was about her. But she had gone over the edge of sleep and she was too tired to come back.

9
The Day

MEG WAKENED in her own bed. She stretched and yawned. Glancing across at Sal still muffled in blankets, she caught sight of Susie and then she remembered. She had gone in last night and asked Mother and Dad to let her have a dog of her own.

Had they said they would?

"We'll manage something," Mother had said.

Would "something" turn out to be Robbie?

Other tag-ends of conversation floated in her mind. Hadn't Mother said, "I never thought she'd be the odd man out"? Meg wondered what it meant exactly, being "the odd man out." Was anybody ever "the odd man in"? And surely Dad had said, "She needs something of her own." Or had he said, "She needs to grow up"? Did they think she would have to be more grown-up before she was given a dog? Or did they think that having a dog of her own would help to make her more grown-up? If only she could ask...

But she could not ask. She had asked out of desperation, in the night. But the Copeland children always waited to be surprised on birthdays. Meg had talked to the other girls at school whose mothers took them shopping and let them choose their own birthday presents. They had seemed to be contented with the arrangement, but Meg was sure it was because they had never been allowed the excitement of a proper birthday. The Copelands always asked each other for birthday lists, but often the presents which turned up at the breakfast table were special things the birthday person had never thought to mention. Two years ago, Meg's family had surprised her with a doll family. She still treasured them. On rainy afternoons, she and Charlotte would sit and make them hold complicated conversations. Dad had given her a father doll. Mother had even made a pair of spectacles for him so that he looked like Dad. Mindy was there with her ponytail. Sal was a little small but she had real wooden crutches which Dad had carved and braces made of pipe cleaners. Meg had taken them off when Sally did not need to wear them any longer. They were all there—Kent, Meg herself and Mother. Meg, who had caught her family busy with pipe cleaners and bits of cloth and wood, had never dreamed that these had anything to do with her birthday.

All she could do was wait. It was a long week. She watched carefully to see if anyone went away for the afternoon. There were no Westie kennels in Riverside. But nobody went anywhere, unless they hurried to get home before she came in from school. She wondered about the sleigh ride too. But on Thursday a thaw set in, and on Friday morning there was no snow left for sleighing.

Then, finally, she opened her eyes to find that Saturday morning had arrived.

When she went to breakfast, her cheeks pink, her heart beating faster than usual, the entire family was gathered, waiting for her. Sally had already sung "Happy Birthday to You" into her ear while she was dressing. Dad had administered birthday smacks on her seat when she passed him on her way to the bathroom. Mother had given her a kiss for every year and "one to grow on" before she combed her hair and slipped on a new pale green hair-band. But still, at the Copeland house, birthdays really began at the breakfast table. It was there that the lucky one faced a pile of mysterious packages. He enjoyed whatever breakfast he chose to name—even waffles or French toast. There, he bore all the teasing and laughter and explaining and exclaiming that are part of present-giving in a large family.

But there was only one box at Meg's place! It was big enough to hold several presents, but the card said merely *Happy Birthday, Meg, with love from Mindy*.

Meg swallowed nervously and began to tear off the wrappings. She pried open the carton. It took her longer because her hands were unsteady. The carton had held their Christmas turkey.

"She's giving you the bird," Kent warned Meg.

"Gobble, gobble, gobble," Sal added.

At last, Meg got it open, and there was a bicycle basket.

"It's just what I wanted," she told her eldest sister earnestly.

She held it high and admired it. But her face felt starched, as though the polite mask she wore might crackle and go limp any moment. There were seven people in this family. What about the others?

Mother leaned over and kissed her suddenly. "Don't worry, darling," she consoled her. "Your birthday is just beginning. Some of your presents are coming later, that's all."

"Your crumpet is toasting," Sal added. "And Mother got runny honey!"

Meg looked at her. Sal met her gaze sympathetically, as though she knew exactly how Meg had been feeling. Looking around the circle of faces, Meg saw that Sally was not the only one. Everybody knew. They were all watching her with anxious, loving eyes. And every one of them was looking excited about something. Even Grandma.

Meg relaxed. "I thought Kent was going to give me this basket," she bragged. "I saw it up in his wardrobe two weeks ago."

"You little demon," Mindy cried. "I hid it there because I thought that was one place you wouldn't poke into!"

Meg flushed. She had not been prying. Mother had sent her in to hang up Kent's white shirt.

"She wouldn't have had to poke to see it, Melinda," Grandma said crisply. "I saw it myself and I only went in to dust the tops of things. You didn't even have it covered."

Last Tuesday afternoon, Mother had sent Meg again with clean clothes to Kent's room. Grandma had come up quickly and caught her arm as she had been about to go in. "I'll attend to those things," she had said.

Bossy, Meg had thought. Mind your own business. "My mother told me to look after them," she had said coldly, and she had swept past Grandma into the bedroom.

Meg had seen the bicycle basket a full week before, but Grandma would have had no way of knowing... Had she been trying to keep Mindy's gift a surprise?

"Here's your crumpet, birthday girl," Mother said, presenting it with a bow.

"And here's the butter." Mindy followed suit.

"And here's the honey," Grandma finished, with a laugh.

Meg had been planning to have strawberry jam, but she spread honey on her crumpet instead. After all, honey was just as good. Maybe better.

All morning she waited for something to happen. Clearly, the entire family was in on some secret. She would not let herself guess. Suppose she was wrong! But suppose, just suppose...!

"Happy birthday to me," Meg sang at the top of her voice.

Noise made waiting easier. Mindy groaned and put her hands over her ears. Susie crept under Sal's bed to escape from the racket. Grandma went into her bedroom and closed the door with a little bang.

"She almost slammed it," Meg thought gleefully—and went on singing.

Time for lunch! Meg scanned her place with eager eyes. Nothing. Knife, fork, spoon, glass—but no sign of a present. She thumped into her chair.

"Not long now, Meg," Dad told her with a twinkle.

"She can have her present from me this

minute," Grandma announced, surprising everyone. "It was delivered this morning. I was afraid it wouldn't get here in time. I couldn't find one in Riverside and I had to order it. It's just inside the front door, Kent."

Kent dashed off, all agog at the mystery. He came back puffing, dragging a narrow box longer than he was. The food grew cold on their plates as the Copelands watched. Grandma had not shared this secret with anyone.

Meg pried open the box at one end and saw with astonished eyes a wad of greenish material, ropes, a pole...

"It's a *tent!*" Kent shouted in amazement and delight.

The Copelands, one and all, turned to stare at Mrs. Kent. Grandma looked flustered under their combined gaze.

"I had a tent once, when I was a child," she said, defensively. "We had it up all summer out at the lake. I decided children couldn't have changed all that much."

Meg sought for words to explain to her grandmother what a perfect present it was, but Kent spoke first.

"It's marvelous, Grandma," he told her. "That's about the best present I ever heard of. Mike and I could sleep out in it..."

"It's mine," Meg snapped at him, holding fast to the box. "Grandma gave it to me."

"Have you thanked her for it, Meg?" Mother asked quietly.

"Thank you, Grandma," Meg said.

The words sounded lame and dutiful. None of the sparkle inside her got into them. She considered going around the table and giving Grandma a hug, but before she made up her mind to do it, the moment passed.

"Kent can lug it down cellar, and the moment the ground is dry we'll put it up for you, Meg," Dad promised.

They ate. Meg, because it was her birthday, did not have to help with the dishes. She went out to the garage to admire her bicycle basket which was now on her bicycle, but it was too slushy to go riding. Besides, Charlotte had had to go out of town with her mother.

"Meg!" Dad called.

She ran back to the house, trying not to hope too much for something special to happen. There stood Mother, Dad and Sal with their coats on. They had that look of bottled-up excitement on their faces which said that the surprise was drawing near.

"Come on, Miss Margaret Ann." Dad took down Meg's coat and held it open for her. "We're going to go and buy you a birthday present."

Meg wiggled her arms into her coat sleeves. Then she looked at them. She could not bear it much longer. She had been waiting so long for this birthday, and by now the day itself seemed to her to have lasted at least a month. Perhaps Dad saw all of this in her face, for he relented.

"Hurry up," he ordered, steering her toward the door, "or your present will grow tired of waiting for you. I haven't met him myself, but didn't you tell me his name is Robbie?"

10
The Gay Young Blade

WHEN THE COPELANDS climbed out of the car, Mrs. Miller was waiting for them.

"How's Susie?" she asked Sal.

"Wonderful," Sal smiled. "I don't know what she's going to think of another dog in the family though," she added doubtfully.

Meg held her breath. Mother had said very little on the way to the kennel. Meg remembered just enough bits and pieces from that night when she had asked for Robbie and then fallen asleep while her parents talked to be almost sure that it was Dad rather than Mother who had thought she should have a pup. Probably Mother was worrying about Grandma. The subject had never been brought up in front of Grandma—at least, not in Meg's hearing—and she was certain that Grandma would be scandalized at the thought of two dogs. Now, if Sal were going to disapprove too, maybe Dad would yet change his mind.

But Mrs. Miller set Sal's fears at rest.

"Several of my customers have bought a second dog, and every time they've told me that though the older one is jealous at first, the pair become inseparable in no time. They're company for each other."

To Meg, it seemed that they stood for hours and hours, talking and talking. Mrs. Miller agreed that Susie might have started chewing things because she was bored and wanted attention.

"A pup may be what she needs," she added. "I have two to show you. You'll want a male."

At last, they started out to the kennels. Meg wanted to run, but they all walked at Sal's pace. Once they were inside the small building where the puppies were housed, Mrs. Miller reached into one of the cages and scooped up a puppy.

"Oh," Meg cried. "That's Robbie!"

He cocked his head on one side and looked at her. He was covered with baby fuzz, very different from Susie's wiry coat. Around his wide, wondering eyes, it seemed to curl. He was not at all afraid. He cocked his head the other way and pricked up his soft ears. He was so small.

"How old is he?" Mother asked.

"Two months."

"You said you had another one," Mother suggested. "An older one?"

"Yes." Mrs. Miller put the little fellow back with his brothers and sisters and turned to the next cage. This time, when she took a pup out, she stood him on the floor. At once he raced away from them and hid behind a stove. In the glimpse Meg caught of him before he disappeared, she saw that he was much bigger than the first one. He had none of the fluffy baby coat. His hair was short and wiry. His ears looked too big. He seemed, to Meg, to have a face like a fox.

"He's five months old," Mrs. Miller said.

"That's better." Mother looked relieved. Then she saw Meg's face. "I'm sorry, Meg, but it's that one or none at all." Her voice left no room for argument. "I know today is your birthday and you should be allowed to choose the one you like best, but you are going to be away at school and I'm going to have to clean up the carpets after him. Susie was already housebroken when we bought her, but we can't expect a miracle like that every time. Remember, in three months the little one will be just the same size as that one."

"But...I wanted a puppy," Meg cried.

"He is a puppy," Mother declared. "When you get him home beside Susie, you'll see what a baby he is. But for goodness' sake, if you don't want him, say so right now. He does seem nervous."

The pup had come out from behind the stove at a dead run. He raced the length of the room, circled, slowed and came to a halt well out of reach, full of curiosity but clearly ready to run. Meg squatted down to make friends. The pup, startled by her shifting position, tumbled over himself in his hurry to get back behind the bulwark of the stove.

"Come on, Wag," Mrs. Miller urged. "He'd soon be used to you," she went on when the pup showed no signs of reappearing. "He is a bit nervous. If it weren't for that, I'd keep him to show. He's a beautiful dog. I'm definitely keeping his sister. But one day about six weeks ago, a woman was in here looking at the pups, and as she turned to go through the door she dropped the heavy purse she was carrying. He was right there, sniffing at her heels. He was the friendliest of the four to begin with. But that purse landed right on top of him. I think he thought the world had caved in on him. Since then, he's been jittery. He's fine with me—but I'm afraid that sometime in the middle of a dog show a judge would move quickly and the pup would forget all his training and jump back or crouch down. Here he comes now. Come on, Wag. We call him Wag, but he's only beginning to recognize it. You could call him whatever you liked."

The pup charged out into the open again. This time, just before he reached them, he skidded to a stop and stood with all four feet stiffly braced. Then he growled.

The Copelands, Meg included, burst out laughing. Even Mrs. Miller, who must have been used to it, grinned. It was the silliest growl they had ever heard. He sounded like a mechanical toy. The growl, which was clearly meant to be enormously fierce, came out like a small, high whir. It almost squeaked.

Meg's heart warmed toward him. She did not want to go home with nothing. Once Grandma had her say, Meg might not be given another chance to choose a dog for herself. Then Sal settled the matter.

"He's goofy," she disapproved. "Susie was nervous too, but she stood and shivered as though she were really frightened. She didn't run all around like that. I don't think she'd like him. He's so…wild!"

How often people had told Meg Copeland not to be "so wild"! And who did Sal think she was anyway, telling everybody what she thought and what Susie would like!

"It's not Susie's birthday. It's mine." Meg's voice was unnecessarily loud. "I like him. Daddy, I want him."

The smaller puppy, standing on his hind feet, peering out at her through the wire, caught her eye suddenly. Meg's heart smote her. He was really Robbie, little and sweet and loving. This

other one, this funny, goofy, foxy-faced dog gal-
loping back into hiding, was not half so sweet,
was not sweet at all. But Mother had made the
rules, and now Meg had committed herself.
There was no going back.

"Fine," Dad was saying. "We'll take him."

"I'm going to name him Robbie," Meg
explained to Mrs. Miller. Mrs. Miller nodded
pleasantly.

"Don't shout, Meg," Mother murmured.

"I'm not," Meg responded, automatically lowering her voice.

"Come on then, Robbie," Mrs. Miller coaxed.

Robbie poked the tip of his sharp nose out
from behind the stove to see what she had in
mind. Mrs. Miller lifted him gently in both
hands. She rubbed her cheek against the top of
his head.

"I hate to let you go," she told him. Then,
speaking now to Meg's family, "But I just can't
give him the attention he needs. I know what a
fine job you've done with Susie..."

Meg's chin went up a notch. Someday, Mrs.
Miller would praise the fine job done with
Robbie. If only... She looked back wistfully as
the others trooped outside. The tiny one, the
real Robbie, was lost in a pile of scuffling little
white dogs. Meg lingered an instant, hoping he
would come to the front of the cage to watch her
go. All at once, one puppy detached himself

from the battle and stood on his hind legs to yip at her.

"Meg!" Dad called from somewhere outside, but Meg was standing stock-still.

"You know me," she told the puppy.

Then the other pups were there, jumping up and down, watching her with imploring eyes, yelping to be picked up. Doubt assailed Meg's heart. Had the first one been Robbie or was he that bouncy one on the end? She took a step closer.

"MEG!"

"Good-bye," she whispered to whichever one he was. "I'm coming," she called.

They were at the door of the larger kennel building. Mrs. Miller led the way into the room where she trimmed and "dry-cleaned" the dogs. While she "tidied Robbie's ears a bit," she explained his eating habits. He had had all his shots. She would send them his papers. He had no kennel name as yet. She and her husband had chosen one, but when they submitted it they learned that someone else had already used it. They had called him Wag, but he had been slow to recognize it as his name.

"What did you say you wanted to call him?" she asked Meg.

"Robbie," Meg answered. She tried to sound sure of her choice, but suddenly she was convinced that Angus or Jock would have been better after all.

"Perhaps we could register him as White Robin," Mrs. Miller mused. "Try calling him Robbie and see what he does."

Meg swallowed. "Hi, Robbie," she said weakly.

Robbie sniffed at Mrs. Miller's hand. He paid no attention to Meg. Mrs. Miller laughed good-naturedly.

"I know what you want," she told him, and she gave him a malted milk tablet. Robbie gobbled it down and looked for more. There on the table, with Mrs. Miller fussing over him and the family standing around watching, Robbie seemed miles away from Meg. She had not once touched his upright ears. Here, away from the tiny pups, he looked smaller, almost lovable if she ever got close enough to him to claim him. She was getting a panicky feeling that they were not really buying him for her at all. He was going to be a playmate for Susie. He was going to be trained by Mother. He was never going to notice that she, Meg, was there.

"I guess now is the time for me to give you your next birthday present," Sal said. She shifted her two crutches into her left hand, and with her right drew from her capacious coat pocket a box wrapped in party paper and tied with a gold bow.

"Wake up, silly," she said, holding it out to her younger sister. For a moment, Meg had been living in a dream and the gift had just been another unreal dream-happening, but the sparkle of excitement in Sal's eyes jolted her awake. Her own face lighted with eagerness, and Mother had to rescue the gold bow as Meg tossed it aside.

Inside was a bright green collar studded with gold knobs and a matching leash. The feel of them in her hands made her believe once again it was her birthday. She looked at Robbie with new eyes. Robbie was looking at her!

"There, he's ready," Mrs. Miller said. "I've had him out walking on a leash a couple of times. He loves it. Mine looks different, but it's funny how they know little things like that. He wants you to put it on, I think."

Robbie moved to the edge of the table. He reached out with one paw, endangering his balance, as though he were trying to beckon Meg to him. He made a little noise deep in his throat.

"He's chirping," Meg thought. She could not remember Susie making that noise at Sal. Robbie was going to be different. He was different already.

Meg's hands shook as she buckled the collar around his neck. She felt him now as he twisted his head to sniff at her inquisitively. He put one paw on her coat sleeve. He nibbled at her wrist. He jumped suddenly at some sound none of the humans heard. Meg, who had been expert at buckling things since she was three, had to begin again.

"Stay still, Robbie," she ordered.

Her voice was as unsteady as her hands. She tucked her chin down as far as she could into her coat collar and avoided meeting the eyes of any of her family. If she had caught Sal's glance, she would have been comforted by the knowledge that at least one person understood how she was feeling. Five years before, Sal had said "I want that dog," even though underneath she had been as unsure as Meg was.

Yet there was a difference. Sal had not wanted any dog. She had been ashamed to admit that she was afraid of dogs, and so she had trailed after her family when they decided to look at West Highland terriers. She had meant to keep quiet and let the others think that she just did not like this particular breed. Then she had seen Susie, shivering, looking as lost and lonely as she herself was feeling, and she had spoken up in spite of her fear. Meg, on the other hand, had never been afraid of any animal. She had asked for a dog of this particular breed. Now she was uncertain not because she was frightened, but because she suspected that this pup she had claimed as hers was not going to turn out to be the dog she had dreamed about and longed for. The leash was fastened. Clutching the loop of it tightly, Meg stepped back. Robbie waved both front paws in the air at once in his desire to get down on solid ground.

"Let's go, Meg," Dad said. "He's paid for. Bring him along."

Meg, holding her breath, biting her lip, and wishing her family and Mrs. Miller would somehow vanish, reached out again and lifted him down. She straightened up, keeping hold of her end of the leash in a hand that was slippery with perspiration. Robbie stood quite, quite still. Slowly, his tail rose to a jaunty angle. Finally, he turned his head slightly and looked up at her, his dark eyes bright with daring. It was almost as though he put himself in league with her, as though he said in some language private to the two of them, "Well, we're in for it now, aren't we?"

"Come on, Robbie." Meg put all the strength and assurance she could muster into those three words. Then she started forward, heading for the car.

His tail in the air, his ears up, his big puppy paws almost swaggering, Robbie Copeland marched ahead of his new mistress into their life together.

11
Hi, Robbie

WHEN THE COPELANDS were about halfway home, snow began to fall in fat, soft flakes. Dusk closed in an hour earlier than usual. Meg and Robbie rode in the front seat with Dad.

Susie frequently rode in the car. The moment they started, she would settle herself on the floor. Each of them had lifted her up onto the seat and urged her to look through the car windows and see the world they were passing. Susie always shuddered, closed her eyes, and scrambled back down to the floor the instant they let her go.

Robbie took an entirely different view of things. He was clearly frightened by the adventure he was having. He panted loudly, and Meg could feel his heart hammering against his ribs at an alarming rate. But he did not want to miss a thing. He kept rearing up on his hind legs and launching himself forward into space.

When he was stretched his full length, his forefeet rested on the dashboard and he could see through the windshield. Meg was worried lest he should miss the dashboard with his paws and crack his chin on it instead, but he always landed safely. When Dad turned on the windshield wipers, Robbie moved his head from side to side as though he were watching a tennis match. He was never content to stay in one position for long, however. He had to keep an eye on everything—the passing cars, a train stringing out across a nearby hill like a necklace of lights, the snow, the strange car in which he was a passenger, and the strange people who had kidnapped him. He climbed on Meg's lap and off again at least a dozen times. He put his paws on Dad's arm as though he were trying to help steer. He jumped down and investigated the place where Susie usually curled up. He stood tall and peered over the back of the seat, growling his funny whir of a growl at Mother and Sal.

"Atta boy, Rob. You tell 'em," Dad laughed at him.

All at once the little dog gave a tremendous yawn, turned around three times and rolled up in a ball against Dad's thigh. Dad took off his glove and scratched gently behind the pup's soft ears.

"You picked yourself a winner, Meg," he said,

smiling at her in the gathering darkness. "He's scared to death of us, but he still has enough spunk and curiosity to want to know what we're up to."

Meg nodded. But she wished that Robbie had chosen to rest his chin on her knee. He had hardly looked at her since they left the kennel. Even when he had landed on her lap, he had always been on his way somewhere else.

"But he's mine," she reminded herself, stubbornly. "He's really mine."

She carried him into the house. He did not like being carried. She had a hard time holding on to him.

Kent opened the door while they were still on the step. "We've been waiting and waiting," he burst out. "Did you... Oh, let's see!"

"Hi, Susie. Yes, I'm home. Really home," Sal said, as Susie gave her a wild welcome. "Look, Susie. Calm down. Look what Meg has!"

Both dogs saw each other at the same moment.

"Put him down, Meg," Dad ordered. "They have to get introduced sometime."

Meg did as she was told. She could not have held Robbie much longer anyway. He leaped out of her arms and landed with his four feet skidding in different directions. Susie stood where she was, apparently too astonished to stir. The smaller dog gathered his feet and his wits

together, and then made a token rush at the
older one. Stopping well out of harm's way, he
gave one of his comical growls.

Susie growled in return, but she was in
earnest. She took one step toward him (Robbie
backed up four) and warned him fairly and
squarely that this house and these people were
hers and hers alone. Robbie wagged his tail
hopefully and chirped at her. Then, to the
amazement of the people watching, Susie
turned and walked away. She did not even look
back at Sally. She just stalked into the living
room and was lost from view. Kent dashed after
her and came back to report that she was lying
on the couch with her back to the room.

"She pretended she didn't know I was there,"
Kent told them. "I think she's mad at you, Sal."

"Oh, my poor Susie," Sal grieved and has-
tened to comfort her. She had not even bothered
to take off her coat. They could hear her
explaining the whole thing in a soft, loving
voice.

"Susie isn't answering," Mindy said with a
grin. "Maybe she doesn't want a friend."

Then Meg had what was the greatest shock of
the day. After all, she had hoped she might get
a dog. The tent had been unexpected, but
Grandma had always given interesting presents—last year, she had sent a basketball
hoop. Kent used it most, but they all had fun

with it in the summer. Now Grandma went down on her knees in front of Meg's pup. (Meg could not remember ever seeing Grandma kneeling on the floor before.) And she held out her hand, without any fuss or bother, and let Robbie take his time investigating her.

"What a lovely dog!" she exclaimed softly. Her eyes took in Robbie's pert face, his straight back, his alert ears, his black button nose, his plume of a tail. "Margaret, he's beautiful. Susie can't help liking him once she has her feelings soothed. What are you going to call him?"

"Robbie," Meg got out. She came close to stammering.

"Hello, Robbie," Grandma said gently, winningly.

Robbie backed away from her. She smelled new. She sounded nice, but he was getting anxious at finding not one familiar person, not one known smell. He growled again, but this time the tip of his tail made a small circle in the air.

"Take him out for a walk, Meg," Mother said, starting for the kitchen. "You'd better keep the leash on until he learns to come to you. The yard is fenced in, of course, but it would be hard to catch him if he ran away from us. Hurry up before he wets on the floor. He's got that look in his eye."

Grandma used Dad's hand to pull herself to her feet. Meg, still in her coat, headed for the back door.

"Just take him around the yard once or twice in case he feels in the mood," Mother said hopefully. "Then bring him in. We're having soup and sandwiches. Grandma has the table all set."

The girl and the pup circled the yard, now covered with fresh snow. Robbie was not in the mood. He did not know this yard. He did not know this girl. He was used to tumbling out into the run with his sister. He was not used to wearing a collar for such a long time.

"Hurry, up, Robbie," Meg shivered.

But her mind was only half on what she was saying.

Grandma liked Robbie! Grandma was really and truly glad that Meg had him. Strangest of all, it was Grandma saying "Margaret, he's beautiful... What are you going to call him?" that had made Meg feel, for the first time, that this queer little dog was really hers. Not Susie's playfellow, not an animal for Mother to clean up after, not even the pup who had cuddled so confidingly against Dad in the car—but Robbie, Meg's Robbie.

Now she jerked on the leash with a firm hand. "You've smelled every tree, bush and stick," she told Robbie. "I guess you aren't going to oblige. Mother is going to be disappointed in you...Robbie. Did you know your name was

Robbie now? Hi, Robbie. Let's go in and get something to eat."

Robbie pranced ahead of her. As she fumbled with her mitten trying to turn the knob on the back door, Meg looked down and saw him clearly in the light streaming out through the window of her parents' room. She recognized the spirit in him which had captivated her grandmother earlier. He was so eager, so jaunty, so thoroughly alive!

"Just wait till Charlotte sees you," she told him. "Just you wait!"

At Meg's place on the supper table lay Kent's presents—a feeding dish which matched Susie's and a slightly used tennis ball which he had found in the drawer of the kitchen table and laid claim to in Robbie's name.

"This is a very doggy birthday, I'm afraid," Mother apologized. "But you did get a tent. And Aunt Polly's letter to me this morning said she had put a parcel in the mail for you."

While they were at the kennel, Grandma had baked an enormous birthday cake. The lights were switched out and Kent carried it in, three layers high and ablaze with candles. The icing was thick and fudgy, Meg's favorite. But for the first time in her life, Meg was unable to give her presents and candle-lit cake her full attention. Robbie, shut up in the kitchen where there were no carpets, was crying. He wanted to go home—and Meg gobbled her cake so quickly that she choked in her hurry to go to him.

He was overjoyed to see her. He had imagined that he was to be left alone for the rest of his life. He licked her hand devotedly, and when she got down on the floor and began explaining that this was home now, he put his paws on her shoulders and washed her face for her with his raspberry tongue. Delighted, she settled herself cross-legged, ready to play with him.

But the door was open and Robbie darted off to explore. He did not go about it sensibly, as Susie had done. He raced around furniture, circling the same chair seven or eight times. He went scooting into bedrooms and hid under the beds. Periodically, he chased up to Susie and attempted to engage her in conversation—but Susie ignored him with a determination which daunted even his high spirits. He jumped onto the couch and stretched out, utterly exhausted. But the moment the family sat back, equally worn out, he was up and off again. Mother tried hard to keep an eagle eye on him, but it was like trying to watch the wind. He managed to wet on the hall carpet twice and on the dining room rug once without anyone catching him in the act.

Whenever Mother discovered a damp spot, Meg and Robbie were dispatched to the snowy yard. Robbie was happy to explore the yard again. He had no idea that Mother was sending him out with a mission.

"He's going to sleep with me," Meg said decidedly, when the time came.

Since Susie slept nightly on Sal's bed, Mother could not object without playing favorites. She did suggest that perhaps both Meg and Robbie would be happier if Robbie slept in the cellar, or at least in the kitchen. Meg would have none of it. Dad brought up the box which he and Kent had made for Susie years before, and they put it between the girls' beds, just in case Robbie did not approve of sleeping at Meg's feet.

Before the night was half over, Meg was wondering if it might not have been better if she had allowed Mother to have her way. Not that she, Meg, was going to back down! She had stated her case and she intended to stick to it. Susie slept with Sal! The only difficulty was that Robbie was not Susie.

Robbie was all over the room. When the light went out, he cried like a baby. After switching it on and off a dozen times, Meg gave in and left it on until Sal came to bed.

"I'm not sleeping with that light blazing in my eyes all night," Sal declared nastily. Susie was still keeping her at a distance and Sal did not like it.

Meg turned out the light. Robbie immediately set up an uproar.

"I want my sister," Meg heard him wail. "I

want to go home to my kennel!"

Meg switched the light on. Robbie blinked and subsided. Sal lay and waited with tight lips. Robbie was now going over the room again, sniffing in all the corners, knocking into the shoes in the closet.

"I like dogs," Sal remarked at last, when Robbie showed no signs of settling down and the light still "blazed." "But he's not a dog. He's a night-owl. Meg, don't just lie there. He's your dog. Do something."

Meg thought furiously. Then she checked and saw the hall light was on, left the door open and turned out the light in the bedroom. Mother had said that Robbie was not to be let out into the rest of the house during the night. Meg pushed him back with her bare foot and managed to shove Sal's dresser across the doorway. Now there was some light in the room. Robbie should be happy. The "blazing" light was off. Sal should be satisfied. And the open door was blocked so that Robbie was penned up in the bedroom. Mother could sleep peacefully.

But Robbie was not happy. He wanted out. Meg caught him and took him into bed with her.

"Sh-sh," she told him, sounding like Mother. "Stay now."

But the moment she relaxed her hold on him, he jumped to the floor with a thud that jarred the things on the dressers. The next minute he was scratching at the barrier, whimpering impatiently.

"You don't have to go," Meg told him crossly, fetching him back to bed again.

"I do so," he insisted, scrambling away from her and throwing himself against the chest of drawers.

"Oh, Meg, DO something," Sal groaned.

Susie slept without a wiggle or a sound, ignoring them all.

Meg gritted her teeth, climbed out of bed, clutched the squirming pup to her and crawled over the top of the dresser. She had forgotten her slippers and the floor felt like ice to her bare feet. Nobody was up. An evening with Robbie had exhausted everyone—except Robbie himself. At the back door, while the puppy panted eagerly beside her, she shoved her feet into her winter boots, pulled on her coat over her pajamas and got his leash.

Outside, she waited for him. Robbie sniffed tree trunks. He rolled in the new snow. He tugged her across to the fence and smelled it from one end to the other.

"Come on, if you're not going to do anything!" Meg snapped at last.

Halfway to the door, she suddenly stopped in her tracks, startling Robbie, who had been trotting along at her side. He looked up at her, his face questioning.

"I'm afraid of the dark," she told him wonder-
ingly. "I've always been scared of the dark ever
since I can remember."

She remembered the hundreds of times she
had wakened in the night and lain under the
covers, her body stiff with terror. Mother had
always told her that she let her imagination
become her master. Thieves were climbing up to
the windows, she would tell herself. That shadow by the door was a kidnapper. She could even
see his mask. Wild beasts prowled across the
floor. Often and often she had taken a deep
breath, gathered together every atom of courage
she possessed and fled through the dreadful
darkness to the safety of her parents' bed.

Now here she stood, in the middle of the
night, all alone in the backyard. If she
screamed, Mother would not even hear her.
Suddenly she felt numb with terror. She would
never be able to take the few steps which would
carry her as far as the house.

Then the puppy beside her gave one of his little chirps. It was too small and friendly a sound
to be called a growl, much too happy to be a
whine or a whimper.

Meg found herself looking up. Above her the
stars filled the night sky with frosty fire. Each
star seemed to be shining straight at her,
watching over her, encouraging her. She had no

idea what time it was, but she was sure all at once that she had never been out this late before.

"It's nearly midnight," she told Robbie shakily. "Maybe it's exactly midnight."

And they went on together, not even hurrying, and reached the house unharmed.

Twice again before morning, Meg scaled the dresser and trekked out into the open with her dog. The last time, the sky was streaked with gray dawn. Meg felt as though she had not slept all night. Robbie was still only interested in sniffing. After the third trip, he at last consented to curl up in Susie's old box and snooze—but only if Meg dangled her arm over the edge of her bed and let him cuddle against her hand.

"Meg, time to get up," Sal's voice sounded from some vast distance.

Meg did not move. Her shoulder was stiff, but she had to leave her hand where it was. Robbie needed it— whoever Robbie might be. Meg was not sure she remembered Robbie.

Then two paws came to rest on the bed beside her. A bright small face poked into hers. A raspberry tongue licked her nose lovingly. Meg opened her eyes just a little and smiled.

"Hi, Robbie," she greeted him.

12
A Different Kettle of Dog

ROBBIE was not a bit tired. He took small running jumps at Meg's bed, but the bed towered above him. He cried to Meg for help.

"What's the matter with you this morning?" Sal asked, as Meg lay unheeding under a pile of bedclothes, her eyes once more closed against the daylight. "You'll never make it to Sunday school at the rate you're moving... Meg, I'm talking to you."

"Mmmm," Meg murmured.

Robbie began to whimper in earnest. He ran over to the door and sniffed the place where the doorjamb and dresser met. With one hopeful paw, he pushed at the crack he discovered, but the dresser did not budge.

"Meg...MEG!"

"What is it?" Meg returned, flopping over so that her back was to the lot of them and their fuss. Even Susie was speaking her mind now.

Apparently she had not understood last night that the stranger was to share her room. Apparently she would have to make it clear to him that he did not belong here. She snarled at him, suddenly and viciously. Robbie, who had been intent on shifting the dresser, yelped with alarm.

"The dogs want out," Sal shouted at her sister. Meg had been irritating before but never, Sal was sure, as irritating as she was at this moment. "*Your* dog wants out...and I can't move that dresser. What on earth made you put it across the doorway like that?"

Enraged, Meg came fully awake. She moved as quickly as a cat. In an instant she was sitting bolt upright, her hazel eyes dangerously flecked with green fire.

"You said 'DO something, Meg,'" she hurled at Sal. "So I did it. And now you have the nerve to..."

"Girls, for goodness' sake, stop arguing and let these poor dogs out," Mother said, appearing on the other side of the dresser and viewing it with some surprise. "What on earth..." she began.

Sal opened her mouth to say that was what she wanted to know too, and Meg prepared to hurl an explanation at the pair of them, when Mother figured it out for herself.

"What a clever idea!" she exclaimed. Sal gulped visibly and stared. Mother went on serenely. "This way you had lots of air circulating in the room and yet you kept Robbie from wandering. Who thought of it?"

Meg was too stunned to take the credit, but Sal said grudgingly, "Meg pushed the dresser across there, if that's what you want to know, but now she won't get up...and I can't move it by myself."

"Poor Meg," Mother said. The sympathy in her voice was real. "I heard you and Robbie up more than once in the small hours. Did you have any luck?"

Meg shook her head.

"No wonder the poor pup wants out of here," Mother said. "Come on, Sarah Jane. Did you try to move the dresser? What's the matter with your muscles? Just lean your weight on it and...PUSH!"

The dresser shifted at once. Robbie instantly trotted out through the gap. Meg, still sitting in bed, watched his disappearance as blankly as she had watched her mother and sister shove back the chest of drawers. Then, all at once, she scrambled out of bed and gave chase. He had her slipper. He could not travel quickly with it because no matter how high he stretched his neck to make himself as tall as possible, still the toe of Meg's slipper dragged on the floor.

Mother caught sight of him the instant before Meg descended on him.

"You shouldn't laugh, Mother," Meg said,

clutching Robbie by the scruff of his neck and reclaiming her property. "Wait till he takes your slippers."

"But he looked so proud of himself! He really thought he was going to get away with it," Mother explained. She came over and bent down to pat the culprit. "I have a queer feeling that we're going to have trouble with you, young man," she told him ruefully. "You're a born clown. Susie was always a lady...almost always...but I have a feeling in my bones..."

Robbie gave her hand a swift lick, took advantage of Meg's attention being elsewhere, twisted free, scooted off down the hall and promptly wet the broadloom.

"Meg, put that animal out," Mother said through her teeth.

This time it was Meg who laughed.

Mother's bones had not played her false. The Copelands had trouble with Robbie from the beginning. When he was called, he hid under chairs. When he learned that people could scoop him out from underneath chairs, he took to retreating beneath the dining room table. When Kent turned his back, Robbie not only stole his new socks but proceeded to eat half of them. He nibbled the tousled chrysanthemums which Mother placed in a large vase in the corner of the living room. He gnawed the corner off *Jane Eyre*. Mindy was inconsolable. And however hard they all worked at keeping track of him, he left several puddles behind him every day.

"We'll have to call him the Phantom," sighed Mother as she sent Meg for a sponge and soapy water. "We never seem to be there when he does it."

When he was let out, Robbie dug through the thin layer of fresh snow and came in with a face like a chimney sweep. He yapped at the neighbor's dog through the fence and disturbed the early morning peace.

Meg spent hours undoing the damage he had done. More than once she bluntly told him that he wasn't worth it.

On that first Sunday afternoon, he escaped through the gate and she had to chase him for half an hour. On Monday there was a thaw, and when Meg came home he was so dirty that she had to take him down cellar and give him a bath. On Wednesday she tied him to the end of her bed so that he could not get into any mischief. He fussed at first, but then he settled down and Meg read in peace until suppertime. It was Sal who discovered that Robbie had been quietly gnawing through a chair leg.

"He's not a dog. He's a beaver!" Kent said admiringly.

Charlotte was sick in bed with the flu. Meg talked to her on the phone. Robbie sat in front of Meg, his head tipped sideways, his whiskers quivering, as he tried to puzzle out what she was doing now.

"He's beautiful," Meg said enthusiastically. "I'd bring him over but Mother says not till you're better. He's so cute, Charlotte. He loves me already...well, sort of like Susie and Sal... Just wait till you see him... It sure is awful at school without you..."

She told Charlotte about school, but for some reason she cut the call short after that. It would be nice when Charlotte could see Robbie—if only Robbie lived up to Meg's description of him.

"Why aren't you a good dog?" she asked, scratching behind his ears. Then, in a whisper so that no one else could hear, she added, "Why aren't you really like Susie?"

Susie had tagged after Sal from the first. "Sally's shadow," Kent had named her. But Robbie was always off on adventures of his own. Meg had given up saying "Robbie, come," because he just didn't. Yet when she sat down on the floor and spoke his name in a certain sweet, cajoling voice, he came tumbling into her lap and kissed her chin with wet devotion.

"I should have named you Goofus," she would laugh, pushing him away.

When they sat down to dinner and both dogs were ordered out of the dining room, Robbie instead hid under the china cabinet just inside the door. They could see him peering out at them, two bright eyes, and a small shoe-black nose which quivered as it caught the fragrance of food.

"He's irresistible," Mother said, shaking her head at him. "But he's certainly a different kettle of fish from Susie."

"A different kettle of dog, you mean," Kent corrected her.

Charlotte was back at school on the following Monday. At four-thirty she went home with Meg.

"You know what—I haven't ever seen your grandmother either," Charlotte said as they neared the Copeland house.

"Haven't you?" Meg tried to sound surprised.

It was surprising that she had managed to get away with it for so long. Grandma had come more than three weeks ago, and in all that time Meg had either gone over to Charlotte's house to play or had pretended she had something to do with Mother. Charlotte's illness had helped. Yet from the beginning Meg had known that the day would come when Grandma and Charlotte must meet.

There was the house.

"She calls me Margaret," Meg mumbled, all at once.

"Hi, Jerry." Charlotte was waving at Jerry Soper, who was pedaling by on his bike. When he disappeared, she turned back to Meg. "What did you say?"

"Nothing."

"But you *did* say something," Charlotte protested. "Something about somebody calling you."

"Never mind," Meg snapped. "Do you want to see Robbie or don't you?"

Robbie met them at the door.

"Oh, Meg, he's gorgeous," Charlotte exclaimed.

But Robbie did not like Charlotte at all. She snapped her fingers at him.

"Here, pup," she called.

Robbie backed away, growling. Charlotte shouted with laughter when she heard his growl. Meg had laughed at him herself, but now she could see that he did not understand Charlotte's hilarity. Robbie stopped growling but Charlotte went on laughing.

Meg grew angry. "Stop it," she ordered. "He's scared."

Robbie was as far away from Charlotte as he could get. His rear was flat against the wall and his feet kept trying to crowd right back through the plaster. This girl was too big, too loud, too rough, too noisy for him. That was the moment Grandma picked to come out into the hallway. She took in the situation at a glance.

"You're frightening him, child," she told Charlotte. "Lower your voice and don't slap your knee like that. Margaret, you should have explained that Robbie is still nervous."

Her cool tone said clearly, "So this is where Margaret gets her unladylike ways!" Meg hoped that Charlotte would not notice. Charlotte often missed things that were left unsaid. She always spoke her own thoughts outright and took it for granted that other people did too.

But Charlotte sometimes saw more than Meg imagined.

"You're scared green of her," she taunted Meg the next day. "I wouldn't let any old cat boss me around like that. Who does she think she is, the Queen? And what does she call you...Margaret! Good morning, Margaret," she mimicked.

Meg stood her ground. She fought to make her face seem unconcerned. If anyone found out how much she hated being called Margaret, she would never be called anything else again.

"I am not scared of her," she said stoutly. "I do whatever I please. And Margaret's my name. Your Aunt Rose calls you Charlotte Mae."

Now Charlotte looked wary. She left the subject of names alone. "I still think you're petrified of her," she insisted.

"Well, I'm not, so there."

"We'll see about that," Charlotte mused, her eyes shrewd.

On Saturday, Charlotte put Meg's boast to the test.

13
Nobody See

"LET'S PLAY Nobody See," Charlotte suggested, the moment she had hung up her coat.

Charlotte had invented this game and Meg loved it, even though she had never been able to play it with a clear conscience. They each took turns daring the other to do something. Meg had had to do such things as untie Mother's apron strings, shut Susie up in the bedroom, or make a sandwich for both of them. The tasks were not difficult in themselves, but the point of the game was to do them without being seen by anybody. Whoever had the first turn had to keep on taking turns until she managed to complete one mission undetected. If you were the chosen one, you ducked into doorways, dove behind curtains, slid silently along walls like a shadow. If one person even glimpsed you, you had to begin again. If you were caught outright, you had to pay a penalty. There was a spice of danger, the thrill of keeping secrets, to the game. And they had never done anything really wrong. As a matter of fact, Meg suspected that Mother more than once had pretended not to notice their comings and goings simply because she understood the rules of the game as well as they did.

"I'll be the queen first," Charlotte said as Meg agreed to play.

They got the special chair they always used for the throne. It had a high carved back and to their eyes looked beautifully regal. It had belonged to Grandma Copeland. They dragged it to a corner of the cellar which was screened by a wall of boxes. Meg ran up and fetched the gold paper crown from the dress-up box.

Charlotte seated herself, put a haughty look on her face, and whispered solemnly, "Loyal subject, I command you to go to your grandmother's bedroom...and take something of hers and bring it back to me, to prove you were there."

Meg knew that Charlotte believed she would refuse to go. Taking something of Grandma's was wrong. What was more, Charlotte knew exactly how wrong it was. In the Copeland family, you never went into someone else's things unless you first had permission. Charlotte had been spending the night once when Kent had taken Meg's colored pencils without asking.

Charlotte had sat in on the heated family discussion that followed and she had heard the rule restated.

But if Meg did not go, Charlotte would never believe it was because of a family rule. In Charlotte's viewpoint, rules were made to be broken. She would say that Meg was scared. And inside herself, Meg knew that this time Charlotte would be right.

But Grandma was out. Meg had seen her leave not many minutes before Charlotte came. She was glad, now, that the game called for whispers. Charlotte would not catch a quaver in her voice.

"Your Majesty, I obey," she said and kissed Charlotte's hand.

Charlotte relented at once. "I'll think of something else," she offered. "I knew you'd do it all along."

But by this time there was no turning back for Meg.

"Meg always tumbles into things head over heels," Mother had said once, "and then she wonders why she ends up with bruises."

"I'm going," Meg hissed—and slipped away from the Throne Room. She stayed hidden at the top of the stairs until she was certain there was no one lurking in the hall. Thank goodness Robbie was not the tagalong type of dog right this minute. She wondered briefly where he was and what mischief he was into. Then, like a ghost, she flitted along the hall to her grandmother's room.

The door was closed. Meg had known it would be. Unlike the rest of them, Grandma always shut her door behind her. Since the day she helped to shift Melinda's things into the basement, Meg had not set foot in this bedroom.

She eased open the door. She expected the room to be empty, but she was weak with relief when she saw, with her own eyes, that there was nobody there.

With her hand still on the doorknob, she hesitated. Should she push the door shut behind her? Suppose Mother walked by and found it standing open. If she heard a noise, she might decide to investigate... Meg closed the door. It latched with a distinct click. Meg jumped, in spite of herself.

There was nothing wrong with the room. It was just an ordinary bedroom full of ordinary furniture. But to Meg, in that first moment, there seemed to be eyes everywhere. The wall was ringed with photographs. There was a row of them on the mantel and three more on the dresser. There were even two of Meg, a baby one with curls and a recent one. The Meg in the pictures did not smile at the Meg who had jumped at the click of the latch.

Meg threw back her shoulders, told herself

not to be silly, and looked around for something to take. She had to hurry, hurry, hurry...but what if she took something and before she could sneak it back Grandma came home and found it missing. The closet! If she climbed up on the shelves inside the closet and took something small and high up, Grandma would never notice. It would take a minute longer, but it would be safer.

Clutching at the smooth edges of the shelves, Meg scrambled up as quickly and as quietly as she could. She reached her right hand above her head into the darkness and felt for something, anything. At last her fingers closed around something small. She had no idea what it was. She shoved it hastily into the pouch on the front of her kangaroo shirt and prepared to come down.

Then she heard the bedroom door open.

"What do you want in here, Robbie?" Grandma's voice inquired fondly.

Meg decided later that she still might have managed to get away safely if it had not been for Charlotte. If she had only kept out of it, perhaps Grandma would have gone right back out to help Mother in the kitchen. But Charlotte, alone in the cellar, had grown bored, and against the rule of the game had followed Meg. She had arrived in the hall just in time to see Grandma turning the knob of her bedroom door. With a bellow, Charlotte charged to Meg's rescue.

"Meg! MEG!" she screamed. "Watch OUT!"

Grandma turned on Charlotte and demanded angrily, "What in the world are you shrieking about?"

Robbie yelped with excitement.

Meg, completely unnerved, lost her grip on the edge of the top shelf and plummeted to the floor, bringing half of her grandmother's belongings down in a heap with her.

Mrs. Kent whirled around and stared at her granddaughter and the pile of things in which she lay entangled. Meg had upset at least four jigsaw puzzles. The pieces, hundreds of them, lay all over everything, like a fall of cardboard snow. Dresses were pulled off their hangers. Meg was sitting on her grandmother's flattened hatbox.

It was then that Meg learned from whom she had inherited her quick, white-hot temper. Grandma jerked Meg out of the debris. "Go to your room this instant," she barked. Her cheeks were pale and her eyes blazed. "I shall tell your mother about this. I shall not only tell her. I shall bring her in and *show* her. And you"—she turned on Charlotte, and Meg was glad to see that Charlotte too was shaking in her shoes—"you get out of this house as fast as you can march. Do you hear me?"

Charlotte, who had seemed fixed to the floor, suddenly took to her heels. She did not even glance back at Meg. In all the time they had known each other, Meg had never seen Charlotte obey an order so promptly. As Meg scurried to her room, she realized with a start that in spite of everything, she had carried out her mission successfully. She could not resist telling Charlotte. She swerved, reached the front door just as Charlotte had wrenched it open, and grabbed her friend's arm. Charlotte tried to jerk free, but Meg held on.

"I got it," she whispered.

Charlotte did not understand at once. Meg, waiting, saw that her friend had been in such a rush that her coat was buttoned crookedly. Then Charlotte's eyes widened. "Really?"

"Honest. I have it right here."

"Boy, Meg," Charlotte whispered, freeing herself at last, "I don't blame you for being scared. Your grandmother is a holy terror!"

"I said *go to your room.*" Grandma's voice stung like nettles.

Meg scuttled into her room and closed the door.

14
Margaret Ann Mellis

ROBBIE was lying in his box, his paws resting on one end of a striped scarf belonging to Mindy. He looked up at Meg proudly, clearly expecting a word of praise.

Leaving the scarf where it was, Meg picked the puppy up and dropped down on the bed with him cradled in her arms.

"Tattletale," she told him, but her voice held no anger and he licked her ear.

She was shaking. She had not hurt herself when she fell, but she had frightened herself badly. It had happened so quickly. One minute she and Charlotte were playing Nobody See as they had done one hundred times before; the next, she had overturned the inside of Grandma's closet, Charlotte had been sent packing, and she was shut up in her room, awaiting sentence.

Robbie climbed over her, discovered a snug

corner at the head of the bed, rested his chin on the pillow and dozed off. A moment later, Meg heard him begin to snore softly, like a little old man.

"Goofy," she murmured, laying one of her hands gently over his paw. His paws were so enormous compared to the rest of him. They were bigger than Susie's already. Touching him, feeling how warm and real and alive he was, steadied and comforted Meg.

Suddenly she again remembered the mysterious object she had stolen from Grandma's top shelf. She fished it out into the daylight and studied it. It was a book—a queer book, with a purple cover which felt something like velvet. Later, Meg learned it was plush. There was no name on the front, no title lettered on the spine. Meg opened it and read in round, careful handwriting:

> *Margaret Ann Mellis,*
> *Rushmere,*
> *Ontario,*
> *Canada,*
> *The World.*

"My goodness," Meg said aloud. Not long ago she had written in one of her own books:

> *Margaret Ann Copeland,*

38 Armitage Avenue,
Riverside,
Ontario,
Canada,
North America,
The World,
The Universe.

Who was Margaret Ann Mellis? Meg turned a couple of pages. It was a diary, a child's diary. Was the child named Margaret Ann? At the top of the first page filled with writing, the author had set the date down in the same round hand. Meg gasped. These words had been written sixty years ago.

June 17, 1904
Today is my birthday. Father gave me a diary. Someday I am going to be a great writer. Or maybe a famous singer. All famous people keep a diary. Father told me so. He showed me one by Dorothy Wordsworth.
I am eleven years old. I have a new middy and skirt.

Meg knew what a middy was. Sally wore one to C.G.I.T. It was like a sailor top.

The skirt is brown. The middy is yellow with a white collar and brown tie. Just wait till Mary sees it! Mary Noble is my best friend. She is

137

away visiting her aunt for the summer. We are having ice cream for supper. I turned the crank on the freezer for Mother.

Meg wondered what turning a crank had to do with ice cream. She had never heard of an ice cream freezer. She read on.

I did not have to help because it is my birthday but there is nothing to do with Mary gone. Nellie Kent is coming over for supper. She wants to be best friends but I still like Mary best. Nellie's brother John is hateful. He calls me "haggy, scraggy, baggy Maggie!"

When I grow up, if I meet any little girl named Margaret, I will never call her awful nick- names. Even Father calls me Maggie sometimes now. I tell him not to but he says he keeps for- getting. He says I do not look old enough to be called Margaret. I think eleven is quite old.

I can't think of anything else to write. We are having clam chowder for supper. That is my favorite dish. Good-bye for now, Diary.

Meg let the book close itself and sat staring at it. Margaret Ann Mellis must be, had to be, Grandma. John Kent was Grandma's husband's name. Meg had often heard about him—only he was a minister with a bushy beard, not a little boy who called names! And Nellie...Aunt Nellie

Kent still lived in Rushmere. The Copelands had visited her several times. Meg had never heard of Mary Noble. Imagine Grandma eleven years old dressed in a yellow middy! And she wanted to be called Margaret! Why didn't anyone think to call her Meg?

Somewhere in the distance, Meg heard the front door open and close. Mother and Dad were home. Meg had been so pleased that Mother had gone out before Grandma came home, but now she could hear Grandma talking and Dad answering. If the eleven-year-old in the book were really Grandma, she had certainly changed in the last sixty years. Meg jumped up, tiptoed quickly to her own dresser and hid the diary safely under a pile of pajamas. She would have to sneak it back into Grandma's closet some-time—but not until she had finished reading it. Maybe it was wrong, but nobody would ever know. Besides, it was so old it was like history.

Dad decided on the punishment. He set up three card tables in a row across one end of the dining room. Meg was then detailed to pick up every single solitary jigsaw puzzle piece and carry them all out to the tables. She was to sort the puzzles out, and in order to do it she would have to put every one of them together.

If Dad had thought about it for a week, he could not have chosen a more horrible punishment, Meg thought, as she dumped boxes full of pieces onto the waiting tables. She had never liked jigsaw puzzles. She was no good at them. Now, every day until each puzzle could be put away in its proper box, she was to spend an hour of her free time working at them.

The first time Grandma pulled up a chair and quietly set to work helping her, Meg was too surprised and flustered to say anything. Grandma did not say anything either. At least she said nothing about the havoc Meg had wreaked in her closet.

"Look for the edge," she advised, skillfully matching two and then three pieces. She stood the four box tops in a row across the back of the tables. Meg gave them a nasty look. Then she saw that the completed puzzles were pictured there—one of some trees ablaze with October scarlet, one of a collie running at a boy's heels, one of a deep blue, northern lake ringed with evergreen, and finally, one of an inn in old England with a coach and horses drawn up at the door.

Meg looked down at the hundreds of pieces of cardboard spread out in front of her. Suddenly, she saw bits of orange... one...two...three... four... Three of them had a straight edge. Two of them fitted snugly together. Delight dawned in Meg's eyes. Clearly, she had found a bit of the autumn picture.

"Good girl," Grandma said, and fitted a third

piece onto Meg's two.

After that, they worked together every day. They did not talk much. Grandma grew too wrapped up in what she was doing to chatter, and Meg was grateful because she was afraid she might let something slip about the diary.

Margaret Ann Mellis had had a dog named U-no. Her cousin Harry had named him that as a joke. When people asked them what the dog's name was, the children answered promptly, "U-no." "No, I don't know," the puzzled questioners would reply in turn. "Yes, U-no," the children would chorus, hugging themselves gleefully at the bewilderment on the grown-ups' faces. Meg thought it very clever of Harry.

U-no was forever in trouble and Margaret was forever getting scolded about him. He dug up neighbors' gardens and got into garbage. He begged tidbits from the lady next door and grew fat. Margaret Ann despaired of ever turning him into a proper dog.

Meg knew how she felt. It was now nearly the middle of February and Robbie was still unhousebroken and disobedient. When he was well-behaved, when he played the clown engagingly, the family petted and pampered him. The moment he left a puddle on the carpet or squeezed through a hole in the fence and disappeared for over an hour or left his tennis ball where Grandma stumbled over it, somebody always said nastily to Meg, "Why don't you train that dog of yours!"

At school, too, Meg knew that things were going far wrong. Not that everything had been fine before, but as report card day drew near, as she tried test after test and left them all half finished, Meg began to be afraid in a way she had never been before. This time, Margaret Ann Mellis was no comfort. She brought home a report card saying she was an honor student and her father put it up on the mantelpiece for everyone to see. Meg wished she knew her secret.

For by this time, she was trying again. Her family did love her. She recognized that she had always known this, even when she had told herself they did not. They wanted her to succeed and she wanted to please them. But she could not seem to help herself. She was so terribly slow. Her thoughts wandered and she did not even realize that she had stopped listening to the lesson until, all at once, the rest of the class handed in their work or shot up their hands for an answer—and she was left behind. The work she finished was nearly always right, but she only made a beginning. Night after night, she promised herself things would be different in the morning. She resolved to work the way Charlotte did. Charlotte was often wrong but she always had her assignments done on time.

But Meg was not Charlotte. Meg still clutched her pencil too tightly and put down each letter too slowly and carefully. Then, while she paused to flex her cramped fingers, a bird would swoop past the window and Meg would begin to wonder about birds, about spring, about anything at all but reading, writing and arithmetic.

Valentine's Day and report card day came together that year. Miss Armstrong's eyes looked sorry as she handed Meg her envelope without a word. Under cover of her desk, Meg took one quick look. Then she stuffed the card into the patch pocket of her skirt.

Charlotte had hers out the moment they left school.

"Mean old thing!" she exclaimed. "She failed me in Writing again. And listen to this. 'Charlotte needs to learn to be neat and accurate.' Not one nice thing does she say!"

Meg made no answer and Charlotte's attention was caught. "Well, let's see it," she invited. "Come on, Meg. Why don't you get it over with? It can't be worse than mine!"

Meg knew that Charlotte would not crow over her. Charlotte's marks, though never good, had always been a shade above Meg's, and Charlotte had always put the entire blame on Miss Armstrong. But this time Meg could not bear even Charlotte's sympathy.

"No." Her refusal was so curt, her face so

tense, that Charlotte was silenced.

"You want to come over and play?" she offered, after they had walked a whole block without saying a word.

"No," Meg said again. Then her voice softened and she gave a small apologetic smile. "Not today, Charlotte. I'll see you Monday."

They waved good-bye and Meg Copeland walked on alone. When she was one block from home, she turned and trudged in a different direction. She did not tell herself where she was bound but her feet took her up the hill to Elsje's home. She stood still at the end of the walk and stared at the house.

"What can she do?" Meg wondered dully.

Her feet, moving of their own accord, went up the path Mr. Jansen had shoveled that morning, climbed the steps and halted, uncertainly, on the door mat.

Meg took off her mitten and poked at the bell. She heard it chime deep inside the house. Footsteps approached. Mrs. Jansen swung back the door and smiled down at Meg.

Meg did not smile back. "Is Elsje home?" she managed.

Elsje had gone skating. She would be back for supper. Mrs. Jansen, seeing the misery in Meg's eyes, swung the door wider open and urged the child to come in.

Meg shook her head and turned to leave.

"Where are you going, little one?" Mrs. Jansen called anxiously after her.

"Home," Meg replied briefly.

There was no life in her voice, but Mrs. Jansen, closing the door against the cold, told herself that the Copelands would soon straighten out the trouble, whatever it was.

Meg walked slowly, but this time she did go home. She could think of no other place to go.

15
Meg's Report Card

SOMEHOW, Meg thought her mother would already know. She expected to be met at the door. She had some vague notion of standing up before a family council and being made to explain. For never, in all her life, had Meg had marks as low as those she had glimpsed in that horrified instant. She had failed, failed in every single subject. Miss Armstrong had written: *I am afraid that Meg will not be able to keep pace with this class next year*. Already, they had decided to fail her.

What would she say when Mother and Dad wanted to know why? How would she be able to bear it if Mother cried? The last time Mother had tried to talk to her about school, Meg had been forced to pay attention for a moment because her mother's voice had broken and tears had shone in her eyes. Mother had blinked them back. Her voice had steadied again. It had sounded the same as always—reasonable, concerned, encouraging. And Meg had felt safe again and had stopped listening.

She opened the door and slid through it, taking up as little space as possible. Sal was there.

"Did you bring home a stack of cards?" she asked.

Meg stiffened. Then she understood. Sally meant valentines. Meg pulled some from her coat pocket. When would Sal remember about report cards? Where was Mother?

Nobody remembered. The rest of the day passed, for Meg, in an agony of waiting. But slowly, as the minutes went by, as she worked on the puzzles with Grandma, cleaned up after Robbie, had her supper, she began to breathe more freely. The other three children were all in high school now. Meg had been too worried about her report card to talk about it ahead of time. The Copelands just did not realize what was in her skirt pocket.

On Monday, Miss Armstrong reminded those children who had not handed their report cards in to get them signed and bring them back tomorrow. Meg's was hidden in the drawer with the diary. On Tuesday, the class went on a field trip. Miss Armstrong forgot all about report cards. On Wednesday, there were still six children who had not brought theirs back. Miss Armstrong was very firm about it. "Tomorrow at the latest," she warned. On Thursday, Meg's was the only one not in.

"Meg, where is your report card?" the teacher asked.

Meg shifted from one foot to the other. She did not look at Miss Armstrong. She lied. "My parents have been out of town...but I'll bring it tomorrow. They'll be home tonight."

"I thought I saw your mother downtown yesterday," Miss Armstrong said. Then, as Meg searched her mind for an explanation, the teacher went on, "But I was in a rush and I couldn't stop to speak. I suppose it must have been someone else. Don't forget, Meg. It has to be in tomorrow or I'll have to call your home."

That night, when Sally was having a bath, Meg shut the door to their bedroom, sat down at Sal's desk and practiced signing her father's name. At last, she was sure she had it right. Trying hard not to cry, she pulled the report card to her and signed *Andrew Copeland* in the space provided. Her hand shook, in spite of her. The letters wobbled and leaned a little sideways. But surely Miss Armstrong would never notice.

What will Dad say next month? a voice inside her asked.

It would be the end of March before the reports were given out again. Maybe in all that time some miracle would happen. Her marks would improve and Dad would understand and forgive her.

The next day, when Miss Armstrong was talking to a visitor from Pakistan who was studying education in Canada, Meg slipped up to the teacher's desk and put the report card an top of a pile of papers there.

"Thank you, Meg," Miss Armstrong said.

Meg went back to her seat. She forced herself to walk all the way without turning her head to see what Miss Armstrong was doing. When she reached her seat, she faced the front again. The two teachers were still talking. Miss Armstrong had not looked at the signature. Meg slumped down in her desk. She was safe.

The weekend passed. Monday, Tuesday, Wednesday and Thursday went by. Meg played with Robbie. She talked to Charlotte. She tried hard to work more quickly. On Wednesday, she stopped looking for some special expression in Miss Armstrong's face, something which said she had discovered what Meg had done. Then, when Meg at last had stopped worrying, it happened. Miss Armstrong kept her after school on Friday afternoon. Charlotte, who had blotted her work badly, prepared to stay too—but the teacher told her to go.

"Meg, I was putting your report card with the others last night," she said quietly, when the two of them were alone, "and I saw that although your father's name was written here, it was not his signature. Perhaps you did not read the report card through. I asked your parents to make an appointment for an interview. I was beginning to wonder what was wrong when I saw this. Have your parents seen your report card, Meg?"

Meg shook her head. She kept her face turned away from the teacher's searching gray eyes. She twisted her hands into a knot behind her back to keep them from trembling.

"Just as I thought." Miss Armstrong was silent for a long moment. Meg gulped. "Meg, I'll give you a choice. I can phone your mother and father and explain what has happened—or I will give you the report card and leave you to do your own explaining. Which would you rather?"

Meg's thoughts jumped back and forth. Maybe if she left it to Miss Armstrong to do for her, they would not be so angry... Then she remembered once, last year, when she had been sent to the store and somehow on the way had lost the money. Charlotte had offered to tell Mother for her. And Mother had been so sorry that Meg had been afraid to come to her herself.

"Don't ever be afraid of me," Mother had said.

"I'll tell them," Meg said gruffly.

Then she could not bear it any longer. She snatched the report card from the teacher's hand and ran out of the room. She grabbed her coat, left her boots behind in the locker, and ran on, splashing through the puddles, cutting across soggy lawns. She had to get home. She had to get it over with.

Just outside the house, she slowed suddenly to a walk. Somewhere, she had to find words before she went in and faced them. If only she had used a pencil, she thought achingly, she could have erased the signature and pretended she was bringing her report card home for the first time. Maybe they would have believed her. Maybe Miss Armstrong would never have found out...

Sal opened the door and called to her. "I thought you'd been kept in again," she said with relief as Meg approached. "It's spring! Isn't it a wonderful day! Do you realize that it will be March the day after tomorrow?"

"What's so special about March?" Mother asked from behind her.

"Why, Mother, didn't anybody ever tell you that spring begins in March?" Sal asked.

Meg stood in the hall. She was still in her coat. She wondered what Sally wanted. She wondered how to begin to tell Mother...

"It's thawing today, Sarah Jane, but we'll have more snow before the week is out," Mother told her. "March is a cold, blustery, unpredictable, difficult month. Spring should, by rights, begin in April."

Sally went on arguing. "You can't see things growing in March, but that's still the month when they wake up and decide to start. If it weren't for March blowing in and telling everything that spring is on her way, April wouldn't find a thing ready... What's wrong?"

Mother was looking at Meg. "Meg...?" she questioned softly. "What is it?"

Tears began to rain down Meg's cheeks. She said nothing at all, simply stood there, crying. Mother took her coat off as though she were a baby.

"Flu begins in February," she told Sal. "Go and turn down her covers and get out her pajamas. This child is going to bed. All right, Meg, stop shaking. And don't cry any more. You're home now. You'll be all right."

Meg was sick. Whether she really had the flu or whether she was sick because she wanted to stay in bed and not have to explain anything to anybody, she herself was not sure. She stayed in bed all day Saturday. Grandma looked in on her once.

"What's worrying you, child?" she said quietly. "Your eyes look like holes burnt in a blanket."

Meg did not answer, but she lay still after Grandma had gone and thought how strange it was that Grandma should be the one to guess she was worried.

On Sunday, Sally got the truth out of her. She

shut the door and came over and sat down on Meg's bed. Meg closed her eyes, but Sal paid no attention.

"Grandma thinks there's something bothering you and so do I," she declared, her voice hard. "Come on. You have to tell somebody. You kept moaning and yelling in your sleep last night. I can go and call Mother if you like…"

"It's in my coat," Meg said at last. "In my coat pocket."

Sal went out and came back with the report card. She sat down again and read it through, every last mark, Miss Armstrong's comment. She even looked at the signature and her face grew puzzled.

"I did it." Meg confessed. Sal still seemed confused, so the younger girl put it bluntly into words. "I signed Dad's name."

Sal looked at her sister, looked once more at the report card, and then folded it and faced Meg again. Their eyes met. Meg felt as though Sal had reached out in that instant and begun to share the enormous burden she had carried so long alone. Now she did not cry. Something in the set of Sal's chin, something steady and kind in Sal's blue eyes, promised her that her big sister would show her a way out of the tangle. She felt as though she had been lost in a dark forest for a long time—and now Sal had come and was going to lead her out of darkness back into the light.

"What's wrong exactly?" Sal asked sensibly. "Don't you understand the work?"

"I'm too slow," Meg burst out, eager to tell the whole truth at last. "Miss Armstrong says I don't pay attention, but I don't mean to start thinking of other things. It just happens. Then the others are finished, all in a minute or two, and I'm still somewhere near the start. I hate writing! We have to hand in papers all the time. That's all we ever do, write, write, write. From the minute we get there till it's time to go home! Miss Armstrong keeps me in to finish, but she says that that wouldn't be fair on tests. And I get mixed up. She says my spelling is terrible. She keeps telling me that Kent was a good speller so why can't I be one too? But I sound out the words and still they're wrong. Even Charlotte spells better than I do and she doesn't bother sounding out. She just guesses. And Miss Armstrong takes marks off for what you don't get done and more marks off for spelling mistakes..."

As the words poured out of her, Meg felt her heart lifting. She wasn't sick any longer. Sally cared. She was beginning to see that Sally had cared all along, that she could have shared her misery with Sal long ago.

"You're always supposed to be so perfect," she rushed on, spilling out everything that had haunted her for so many months. "Susie is a perfect dog...and Robbie is so bad... Everybody keeps saying what a wonderful, brave sister you are...and you work hard in school...and you always know what to say... and nobody gets mad at you... Everything I do comes out wrong, even when I try to change it!"

After her outburst, Meg felt spent. A silence grew up between the two girls. Sally seemed lost in thought. Just when Meg was beginning to be afraid that things were not going to straighten out, that she had again said more than she should have, Sal began to speak slowly, as though she were examining every word before she let it go.

"Meg, it's not you. It's not me either, though you almost made me think it was. It's just that you need some help. I feel, right now, that I have not been a good sister to you—but you didn't seem to want me to. You'll be surprised to know that this very same kind of thing happened, long ago, when I was ten and Mindy was thirteen. She seemed to be always bossing me and I grew angry—and we were no help to each other at all. But then, one day, we talked and things began to be all right again... I think things can be put right for you, and if you want me to, I have an idea I can help you. Do you really want help?"

Two months before, even a month before, Meg

would have snubbed Sal for suggesting such a thing. But now, she knew how desperate her need was, how helpless she herself was to meet it. Miss Armstrong had already decided that Meg could not pass. Her comments went on: *I would suggest private tutoring, but I know of nobody who could give Meg enough time and I suspect we have left it until too late.*

"It's no use..." Meg began, but she stopped herself.

"I do want help, Sally," she said humbly, "but Miss Armstrong said it wouldn't do any good."

"Ah, but Miss Armstrong doesn't know Elsje!" Sal said mysteriously.

16
Sally to the Rescue

SAL PAUSED suddenly and asked, "You're well now, aren't you?"

Meg sat up and stretched out first her arms and then her legs. She moved her head from side to side, experimenting. Last night, she had had a fever. When Mother had brought her supper on a tray, she had turned her face to the wall. At the very smell of food, her stomach had turned a somersault. Her head had ached. She had ached all over. Her eyes had felt heavy and hot, her hands and feet clammy. Now it was over. She was "hungry as a hunter," as Grandma always said. She could not find an ache anywhere.

"I feel fine," she admitted, her voice tinged with surprise.

"Oh, you weren't just pretending, if that's what you're wondering. Your temperature was over a hundred degrees. I saw the thermometer.

Maybe you did get a touch of flu from Charlotte…although that was quite a while ago. But worrying made you worse, I guess. And now, unloading your worries has cured you. I'm going to have quite a time convincing Mother that you're well enough to come out with me though." Sal shook her head at the prospect.

"I could get dressed…" Meg suggested.

"That's a good idea. Wash your face. Use cold water so your cheeks will have a healthy glow. And comb your hair. Put on your yellow hair-band," Sal threw advice over her shoulder as she started off to talk with Mother.

Meg hustled. When Mother and Sal came back, she was just putting on the yellow hair-band. Never before had she washed and dressed in such record time.

Mother looked dubious.

"But she feels fine," Sal insisted. "And…well, I'll tell you this much. She's been anxious about something, and now we need Elsje's help on a scheme I've thought up. I promise, if you'll let her come with me, I'll bring her back even healthier than you see her now—and tonight I'll tell you the whole story. Come on, Mother."

"Please, Mum," Meg put in.

Emily Copeland smiled into the two faces, so unlike and yet both so pleading, so young. If Sal were somehow going to help Meg, if Meg were, at long last, willing to be helped…

"You be back here in one hour," she ordered, giving in.

Grandma followed them to the door.

"You're pretty smart, aren't you, Grandma," was all Sal said.

Mrs. Kent did not press her for details. "Are you sure you're warm enough?" she called after them.

"Perfectly," Sal called back. "We both have spring fever."

Meg suddenly remembered words she had read in a stolen minute a few days before.

Father says I have spring fever. I don't care. The weather is wonderful. The sun is so bright and there is only a patch of snow on the north side of the house. Soon, soon, soon, I will be able to stop wearing this horrid waist and long, hot, scratchy stockings Aunt Janet knit. I wish Mother would let us go to school barefoot. Lots of other children do but never the Mellises. One of these days, I am going to hide my shoes by the gate on the way to school and then put them back on when I come home. Nellie will tell though and Mrs. Kent always tells Mother anything Nellie says. John is the only Kent who can keep a secret.

I wonder if she ever really did it, Meg thought. And when Sal turned and blew a kiss back to Grandma, Meg followed suit. Grandma had turned to go back into the house. She did not appear to have seen Meg's gesture. It was half-past four. Usually, about now, Meg and Grandma were bent over their muddle of puzzles. She would work at them after supper instead, but an unexpected loneliness caught her heart for a moment as she hurried away at Sal's side.

Sally explained the situation to Elsje in detail. She produced the report card and let Elsje study the marks and Miss Armstrong's comments.

Elsje Jansen examined them carefully. Then she looked squarely at Meg. Meg faced up to Elsje's candid gaze as steadfastly as she could. For a moment, hope deserted her. What could Elsje do? Elsje was just another girl. Miss Armstrong was so certain...

Elsje was old beyond her years. She saw Meg's eyes grow suddenly dull. She saw the younger girl's shoulders droop as though Meg were too tired to hold them back. She saw the sadness tugging at her mouth. Elsje recognized the feeling of defeat which had overpowered Meg. She had met despair like this before. Her brother Piet, who had had rheumatic fever, had been slow to adjust to living in Canada because he had had to spend his first months there lonely and ill. He had been without hope too.

The Jansens at one time had been on the brink of returning to Holland because Mrs. Jansen and Piet had given up trying to begin new lives. It had been Sal's courage which had saved the situation. Elsje could not help but know that she herself had had a great deal to do with inspiring that courage in Sally, but it had been Sal, crippled herself, who had been brave enough to stand up to life and then, impulsively, to offer Piet a chance to do the same. Today, Piet was a friendly, happy boy, at home with himself and his world. And now at last, she, Elsje, was being given the opportunity to do something for Sal in return.

"Talk to her," Sal urged.

But Elsje knew better than that. Listening helped more than lecturing. She made Meg go through it all again, why she had failed, why she was slow, how she had tried to help herself. She had Meg sit down and write a couple of sentences and do a row of adding and multiplying. When she saw Meg struggle over each letter, and then afterward saw what had come of all that laborious work, she whistled between her teeth. Meg wrote jerkily and her spelling was disgraceful.

They made plans, then Meg was frightened when she realized how concrete Elsje's plans were. There was no vague talk of "trying to do better." There were no ifs, ands and buts, no room left for excuses. If she, Meg, worked hard enough and fast enough so that Miss Armstrong would dismiss her at four o'clock with the rest of the class, Sal and Elsje would give part of every afternoon to helping her. They would help her with her schoolwork and they would help her to train Robbie.

"How did you know about Robbie?" Meg gasped.

Elsje grinned. "You told me yourself," she answered coolly.

Meg had only said, "And then there's Robbie... I do everything wrong with him too..." At the time, Elsje had not even appeared to notice.

"I think maybe he is the straw that is breaking the camel's back," Elsje explained. She laughed at Meg's confusion. "We will have a Pooch Academy for just one pooch."

Training Robbie would take fifteen minutes a day. Schoolwork would take an hour. If Meg did not care enough to work hard, Elsje said quietly, she and Sal had other things they could be doing instead. This schedule would mean that they would have to leave their homework until after supper.

"We just got a television," Elsje went on. "But helping you is more important—if you are really going to work."

Meg had heard of how, long ago, people had

been imprisoned in stocks in the public square. She had tried to imagine what it would feel like to be tied hand and foot while people stood and stared at you and talked about you. Now, caught under the eyes of the two older girls as they made up their minds whether she were really worth so much trouble, Meg knew how dreadful a punishment the pillory had been. She agreed to everything they asked of her. Elsje had no idea what would come of it, but as they set the time and decided where to work, she saw hope begin to invade Meg's heart again. Her chin came up. She even grinned. It was not the cheeky grin of the old Meg, but both Sal and Elsje were pleased to see it. Tagalong Maggie was dearer to them than she ever guessed.

That night Sal showed the report card to Mother and Dad.

"I'll explain that you were going to do it yourself," she told Meg. "But I want to tell them about the plans we've made—and I can make them understand better without you there."

Andrew and Emily Copeland listened.

"Poor Meg," Mother said softly, thinking back and recognizing for what it was the fear that had been haunting Meg's face for the last week.

Sal went over every detail of their plans with her parents.

"I know you'd get her a tutor," she said, "but when Mr. Willoughby tutored me in Latin, he said that what I really needed was some help every day. A couple of hours a week was not nearly enough. When Elsje and I started doing our homework together—and Elsje made me work everything out for myself, and then showed me what needed more work —that was what really helped me. If Meg was behind in one thing, if she just did not understand arithmetic or something like that...but from what Miss Armstrong says and from what Meg says herself, no one subject gives her all that trouble. She's a terrible speller. But apart from that, she's slow and she can't concentrate."

"If we had her tutored," Dad said, "she could understand everything she was taught—and still be too poky to finish a test in school. If you and Elsje are willing to take it on, I think we should let you try. We'll explain your ideas to Miss Armstrong. I have a watch with a second hand. That might be of some help. You're welcome to it. It's an old pocket watch of my father's."

"We'd better call off the jigsaw puzzles," Mother said thoughtfully.

"No, don't," Sal protested. "She still has time enough and I have a feeling they might help her. Grandma doesn't let Meg's thoughts wander. I've watched them. Grandma keeps asking her for certain pieces. They're beginning to know each other. I think Meg maybe likes doing it by now, although she wouldn't admit it. And she likes Grandma a lot better. Of course, she doesn't like her all the time," Sal added honestly. "Grandma doesn't mean to pick on her, but she does it just the same."

"You're a smart man," Mother teased Dad. "I suppose when you said she'd have to sort out those puzzles you knew all this was going to happen. I've noticed it myself. Meg and Mother are really starting to appreciate each other. Sometimes I've seen Meg looking at her in the funniest way, almost as if there's something...I don't know...surprising about Mother."

The three of them puzzled over it for a moment, but they had no way of guessing Meg's secret. Even Sal had never discovered the diary which Meg kept meaning to return but never did.

While she waited for Sal to come back, Meg had it out. At that very minute, she was enthralled by a new discovery. (Grandma had not written in her diary every day. There were only fourteen entries in the year she was eleven. When she was fourteen, she had not written a word. But when something exciting happened, she had usually remembered to write it down.)

Meg was near the end of the diary when the seventeen-year-old Margaret Ann Mellis wrote:

Regina, Saskatchewan

*I arrived here the day before yesterday to visit
my Western aunts and uncles—and today, the
house was hit by a tornado.*

*It was stormy all morning. We went to church.
Uncle George has a car but he never drives it on
Sunday. After lunch, we went out on the veran-
da to look at the clouds. A Mr. Williams was
here for the day and he said, "Look at that
cloud! It looks like a cyclone."*

Uncle George laughed at him.

*"You come from the States where they have
such things," he said. "We don't have anything
like that up here."*

*But it came closer. It was the eeriest-looking
thing I ever saw. It was like a long, snaky col-
umn of smoke, spreading up and over the sky. It
began to hail all at once and we took turns running out in the yard to see who could get the
biggest hailstone. They were enormous, like golf
balls. Maybe even as big as eggs.*

*Then Aunt Gladys said, all in a fluster, that
she did not care what Uncle George said, she
wanted every single one of us to go down cellar.
That cloud looked as though it were rolling
straight toward our house. Even Uncle George
didn't object much. By now the whole house was
creaking and groaning with the force of the
wind. We huddled down there like a bunch of
sheep.*

Then there was a great smashing sound and Uncle George started for the stairs. But Aunt Gladys just clutched onto his sleeve and begged him to stay. She looked terrible. Her eyes glittered and her cheeks were as white as paper. I could feel my legs shaking and I kept wanting to sit down but I had on my Sunday dress and I didn't dare. After what seemed like hours and hours, we could hear, even down there, that the crashing and the banging had stopped and that the wind had gone down. So we crept up—and the entire roof had blown clean off the house and was lying across the street.

Inside the rooms, it looked just as though somebody had taken a giant spoon and stirred everything around. The bathtub was in the living room. The windows were all broken. A kitchen chair was sticking halfway out through one. Aunt Gladys and the men made us sit still on places they'd cleaned off while they went after all the shattered glass. I felt old enough to help but I was glad to sit down. Aunt Gladys cut her hand but not badly. I found my diary still safely in my trunk but my trunk was under my cousin Doris's bed and the bed was all in pieces.

We are staying over at Uncle Jim's and Aunt Martha's tonight. They took us all in. The little ones are sleeping on blankets on the floor. Uncle George has been out driving all day, helping people everywhere. This is the first time he has ever driven his car on Sunday—but he has not had one puncture although lots of other cars cut their tires on glass. Aunt Gladys says that the Lord is taking care of him and I think she must be right. I am worn out but I had to write this down. I am so glad I came out West.

Just wait till I tell John Kent. He boasts about the time his grandfather's barn was hit by lightning—and he wasn't even there till it was over. This has been the most exciting day of my life.

Meg heard Sally coming. She darted to the drawer and shoved the diary out of sight. Sally, coming in to tell her what Mother and Dad said, thought, How hard it must have been for her, waiting alone all this time. Her cheeks look so hot and her eyes are terribly bright. I wonder if she's been crying.

"Everything is all right, Meg," she said hastily. "Mother is coming in in a minute."

But Meg, just at first, hardly took in her sister's words. She was still out in Regina with Margaret Ann Mellis, going through the tornado of 1910.

17
Spring Begins

IF IT HAD not worked the first day, it might never have worked at all. But, as Meg went out the door with her report card properly signed and ready to hand in, Sal stopped her and warned in a low but decided voice, "Elsje and I will be here at a quarter after four—and we expect you to be here too. Don't dream about it. Concentrate on making it."

Meg worked as she had never worked before. Several times Charlotte looked across the aisle, her eyes puzzled, to see Meg's pencil flying, Meg's face grim.

"You racing to meet a deadline?" Charlotte whispered when she had a minute. She and Meg had picked up the phrase from Mr. Russell, and in the past they had used it to describe other members of the class.

"Yes," Meg returned, not looking up or pausing for an instant.

Miss Armstrong was delighted and made a point of saying so. Meg's spelling still came back with fourteen out of twenty wrong, but this time she had tried all twenty words. And her arithmetic was not only finished—it was perfect.

It was not hard, that first day. The thought of Sal and Elsje waiting for her was so new and different that Meg felt full of hope and determination. To crown the day, for once her hopes came true. When she arrived, panting and pink-cheeked, Elsje and Sal were both there. And they had worked out her schedule.

"Two teachers at once would get her confused," they had sensibly decided. First, Elsje fired arithmetic facts at her. Then she made Meg work problems out of an old arithmetic text. They timed everything she did. Then they made her do it over again. The second time, she almost always beat her own record.

Sal helped her with spelling and writing compositions. Meg had always had trouble writing stories, but all at once they seemed to come much more easily. Neither Sal nor Elsje guessed that this was partly due to the way another girl named Margaret Ann had once written about herself and her thoughts sixty years before. Margaret Ann Mellis wrote simply, naturally, interestingly of her best friend, her tent, her birthday. Meg wrote of Robbie, of

Susie, of Charlotte, of jigsaws. Sal allowed Meg to choose her own topic and then gave her ten minutes to write down something about it. When the ten minutes were up, Meg was supposed to have at least five sentences on paper. Meg, imitating Margaret Ann, told about herself, and Sal was astonished at her sister's skill, even while she deplored her spelling.

Dog-training came at the end when Meg was weary of sitting still. And, surprisingly, training Robbie turned out to be a delight. Even Sal and Elsje, fond as they were of their own dogs, admitted that Robbie learned with uncanny quickness. He was so eager to please. Susie had continued to ignore Robbie for that first week. Apparently she had had hopes that he might yet vanish if she paid no attention to him. But by now she had reluctantly decided that he was here to stay and it was up to her to bring him up in the way he should go. She was an old hand at "Come" and "Sit," and she helped Meg enormously, roaring reprimands at Robbie when he made a mistake, and executing all the orders with him so that he had her example to follow.

"Robbie, stay," Meg would command—and Susie not only stayed, sitting exactly as she should, but she growled at Robbie until he meekly stayed too.

"Robbie, come," Meg ordered firmly.

Susie came obediently, barking back at Robbie something which sounded like "Get up and get over here, you numbskull."

Robbie delighted Meg by fetching things naturally, catching onto the game the moment a stick was tossed for him, racing back with it in his mouth and putting it into her hand. Susie had never learned to fetch anything. Meg felt positively smug about her dog.

At supper, on that first night, Sal startled Meg and everyone else by announcing that she had discovered her younger sister to be a budding genius.

"Listen," she invited. She read aloud:

I have a Westie named Robbie. He is a great nuisance to me because when he should act like a dog he acts like a clown instead. When he is good, everyone says, "He is as cute as a bug in a rug." But when he leaves a puddle on the rug, everyone says, "Oh, that dog of yours!" He thinks he is king of the world. He even tried to fight a Great Dane once but the Great Dane only fought with dogs his own size.

As Meg sat blushing, listening to her own words, they sounded all wrong. She had not come close to capturing Robbie on paper. But the Copelands, and Grandma too, laughed and applauded.

"You're in print, Robbie," Dad said to the whiskers under the china cabinet.

Like a bulb which has been buried in the earth and suddenly awakens to the fact of spring, pride in herself stirred within Meg, and she felt as though she might be going to burst into flower.

All the days were not as good as the first. Sometimes, in spite of her good intentions, Meg daydreamed and had to stay in. How she dreaded coming home late and facing the reproach in Sal's blue eyes! Even Robbie came to depend on her. Mother told her that promptly at ten after four he would run out to the front window and jump up into a chair beside it from which he could see Meg coming. When she failed to come, he cried until Mother threatened to stuff her ears with cotton.

Sometimes Sal grew impatient when, after days of drilling, Meg spelled "there" t-h-a-y-r or "too" t-w-o. But Elsje, who had worked for so long with dogs and who had struggled for months to help Piet, never lost patience. Among them—Sal with her anxious love, Elsje with her steady, hardheaded faith and Robbie with his eager devotion—they kept Meg working.

March passed. The jigsaws were done and put away. Meg looked so wistful that Grandma went downtown and bought another one with one thousand pieces. She set up the card table again, a little shyly, and started working at the puzzle without saying a word. "Hurrah," Meg said, and joined her whenever she had a free minute.

The days grew warmer, although every time Sal was certain spring had come to stay the wind blew the warmth away the next morning. Robbie could now run free in the park. He came speeding right to Meg the instant she called his name. He learned to shake hands—and then he was forever sticking his paw up at them, hoping that somebody would think to reward him with a biscuit.

One morning, Meg woke up to find Robbie sound asleep on the bed beside her. Not only was he on the bed, he was sharing the pillow! Meg did not tell her mother. Robbie still wandered about the room at night, but more and more often, he finally settled down next to his mistress.

Then the end of March arrived. Miss Armstrong handed out the report cards again. She smiled at Meg, but Meg did not smile back. She was too worried.

This time, she did not look. Charlotte was dancing along the sidewalk. The Easter holidays were beginning. They were free for ten whole days. The thin March sunshine spilled into the street, lighting up the bare trees, drying the sidewalks. Charlotte was wearing knee socks and her spring coat.

"Yippee!" she sang, whirling around and bumping into Meg.

Meg went stolidly on. Charlotte stopped cavorting to stare at her friend. Over the last few weeks, the two girls had not seen much of each other. Meg had tried to explain her new schedule to Charlotte. Charlotte had been impressed. She had also been horrified when she saw Meg battling with her work. It seemed to her as though Sal and Elsje between them had robbed Meg of laughter. Before the report cards were given out, Charlotte had resolved not to ask Meg any questions this time. It would be dreadful if, after all she had done, Meg's marks had not improved. But Charlotte could not stay quiet any longer.

"Meg, it can't be that bad!" she said, echoing the words she had used a month and a half ago. "What did you get?"

"I don't know," Meg answered, her voice taut with strain. "I didn't look."

"Are you crazy?" Charlotte wanted to know. She stood stock-still on the sidewalk, but Meg went doggedly on and Charlotte had to run to catch up.

"Don't talk about it," Meg ground out. "I don't want to talk. Let's just get home."

Then she began to run. Charlotte huffed and puffed along at her side.

"Stop," she panted at last. "I can't run another step."

Meg ran on, leaving Charlotte behind.

"I can't wait," she called over her shoulder.

She was home. She turned in at the walk, raced up to the door, burst into the kitchen. There they were: Mother washing the tea dishes, Dad home early because tomorrow was a holiday, Grandma knitting a sweater for Jane Preston, and Sal and Elsje arguing over an English assignment.

"I...have...my...report," Meg puffed. Her hand shaking, she held it out to her father.

It took him an eternity to get the envelope open. He pulled out the card and a letter. He unfolded the letter first. Then he looked around at the circle of intent faces.

"This concerns all of us so I will read it aloud," he said.

Meg tried to hush the clamoring of her heart. Her pulse drummed in her ears. Her breath came in ragged gasps. But she heard. She heard, and her heart flooded with joy.

Dear Mr. and Mrs. Copeland,
When you told me of your plans for Meg's studies, I admit I was skeptical. I was sure that children would not have the stamina to keep working at such a long-term project. As you will see, when you examine this report card, Meg's marks

*have come up in every subject but Spelling. I
have even seen some improvement there in her
work in class. She has not yet made a passing
grade in Spelling or in Writing. Her marks are
still borderline on most of her subjects. But she
has tried so hard that on our last tests she finished all but one and she was only two problems from the finish on that. She still has the
ability to do much better work than she is
doing, but I wanted you to know that I can see
no reason for her to be retained in this grade if
she continues to work as she has during the
past four weeks. May I congratulate you on the
help you have given her.*

Sincerely,
SANDRA ARMSTRONG

Charlotte came banging into the room just as
he finished reading.

"What's everybody crying for?" she demanded,
her voice sharp with concern. "What did Miss
Armstrong say?"

"She said I have two fine daughters," Dad
said, his voice very deep. "But she's not half as
proud of them as I am."

"Of Elsje too," Mother added softly, her face
shining.

"Amen to that," Grandma said, wiping her
eyes unashamedly on Jane's sweater.

177

18
Margaret

HALF AN HOUR later, when the two girls were in Meg's and Sal's room, with Robbie keeping them company, Charlotte said, "What shall we do? How about Nobody See?"

She was teasing, but Meg flushed. A little of the wild happiness inside her died. Charlotte, seeing she had said the wrong thing, asked, "What did the old witch do to you for knocking all that stuff down? You never told me. I'll bet you got skinned alive!"

It was then that Meg reached into her dresser drawer, right in front of Charlotte, and took out the plush-covered diary.

"She's not an old witch," she said, wondering when she herself had changed her mind about her grandmother.

Charlotte looked skeptical.

"Oh, she's bossy sometimes and she always wants to know everything we're doing and she... Well, I guess we bother her too." Meg tried to make it clear. "I was named after her," she added unexpectedly.

There was pride in her voice. Charlotte looked bewildered. "But she calls you Margaret—and you hate it. I know you do."

"Come on," Meg ordered, not bothering to answer.

She led the way to the kitchen, where Grandma still sat, close to the window so that she could get the late afternoon light and "save electricity." Her knitting needles were clicking busily when the two girls approached. Jane's sweater was a gay red with a girl skiing on the back. Not many days before, Meg had eyed it angrily, sure that Grandma was being unfair knitting for Jane who was hundreds of miles away while Meg, right in the house with her, had no sweater like that. Now she did not think about it.

She paused and looked at her grandmother through Charlotte's eyes for an instant. Such a little while ago, she had seen Grandma this way herself. Here was the woman who called her Margaret when she wanted to be called Meg. Here was the woman who had moved into her house and made it impossible for her to have her own room. Here was the woman to whom she had had to apologize more than once, who had sent her to her room, who had often made it awkward for her to talk to Mother alone, who sometimes made a hard note sound in Dad's voice. Grandma was old and fussy and bossy and she nagged. If you did not let her help, you hurt her feelings. If you asked her to help, it was always when she was tired or when she was making a point of "not interfering." She was an extra person in the house. She had, somehow, changed the shape of their family.

Yet, although Meg saw all of this, now she saw much more. She saw the woman whom Sally had kissed so warmly, the woman who had sat beside her looking for the "corner piece" by the hour, the woman who had had to leave her home, which had been for years without children, and come to be part of a family with three girls and a boy, the woman who had helped her to feel that Robbie was really hers, the woman who had once been a girl like herself, even like Charlotte, a girl who cranked the ice cream freezer, who got knocked over by a horse, who loved sleeping in a tent, who wanted to go barefoot in the spring, who had been in a tornado...and Meg knew that Grandma was lonely. In the days when she, Meg, had been at odds with everybody, she had learned what loneliness was like.

She took a step forward and held out the diary.

"I took this out of your closet, Grandma," she

said steadily, "that day when I knocked the puzzles down. I'm sorry I took it without telling you, but I'm glad I read it. It was the most exciting, the best book..." Meg ran out of adjectives.

Grandma put down her knitting slowly, but it was a minute before she took the little book. Still not saying a word, she opened it gently and turned one page and then another. Meg waited, but when Grandma let the diary close itself and lie shut in her lap and there was still silence between them, she gulped and went on bravely.

"You've never really met my friend Charlotte, Grandma. I mean... I know you know who she is...but she's my best friend. We're like you and Mary Noble...Charlotte's like Mary...and I wanted you to know her."

Meg heard her own voice trail off lamely. Charlotte was glaring miserably at her and Grandma did not seem to understand.

"Come here, child," Grandma said suddenly, reaching out a hand to Charlotte.

Charlotte hung back uncertainly, till Grandma repeated firmly, "Come here. I won't bite you."

She drew Charlotte forward into the light falling through the kitchen window and studied her. Charlotte, tongue-tied for once, was staring down at Jane Preston's sweater as though she were counting the stitches.

"I haven't thought of Mary Noble in years," Grandma mused, giving Charlotte's hand a comforting pat. "But I remember her. You're not really like her. Mary was thin and gangly. She had thick black braids. When she was fourteen she could sit on her hair!"

Charlotte was looking at Grandma now. Meg saw the tightness go out of her friend's shoulders. Charlotte was waking up to how interesting a grandmother could be.

Suddenly Robbie bounded up to Meg and dropped his tennis ball squarely at her feet. As Meg whispered "Good boy" and bent to pick it up, she almost missed Grandma's next words.

"I'm so glad Meg has you for a best friend, Charlotte," Grandma said warmly.

Meg!

Meg straightened abruptly. She stared at her grandmother.

Grandma was looking self-conscious, all at once. It was a moment before her eyes met her granddaughter's.

Meg smiled at her suddenly. She felt free, grown-up, wonderful, as though the world belonged to her and she could give it away to anyone she pleased.

"You can call me Margaret, Grandma," she said.

JEAN LITTLE

Mama's Going to Buy You a Mockingbird

**Winner of the Ruth Schwartz Children's Book
Award and the Canadian Library Association
Book of the Year for Children**

Jeremy is not having a good summer. His best
friends have moved away, and he has to stay at
the cottage with only his little sister and his
Aunt Margery. His parents have remained in the
city so his father can have an operation.

When Jeremy finally sees his father, he finds
out that he has cancer and that he isn't going to get
better. Suddenly, everything is different.

Then Jeremy finds an unlikely friend in Tess,
who also knows what it's like to lose someone. And as
their friendship grows, through good times and bad,
Jeremy discovers that his father has left him something that will live forever...

"...a moving, sensitive and psychologically sooth-
ing novel about one family's response to death."
— *The Globe and Mail*

A PUFFIN BOOK

J e a n   L i t t l e

★ **STARS COME OUT WITHIN** ★

In this new volume of memoirs, Jean Little continues her life story, begun in *Little by Little*. Hers has been a charmed life in many ways — full of family and friends, laughter and accomplishment. Yet her life also has a dark side. We share her shock as she loses one eye to glaucoma and later the sight in her "good" eye as well. She battles depression as she adjusts to her new limitation.

Then she discovers two blessings. One is a computer that talks; the other is her seeing-eye dog, Zephyr. She tells movingly of the freedom and love Zephyr brings her, and of an unexpected crisis they face together.

Through it all, Jean Little is sustained by the strength of her remarkable mother, and the companionship and patience of close friends. This is an honest, funny, emotional story of a woman learning to make light of darkness.

"*Stars Come Out Within...* is about courage and perseverance and one indomitable human spirit. And Little's unforgettable writing style will make you laugh and cry at the same time. It's a lovely book that should be must reading, for people of all ages."
— *The Toronto Sun*

A **PUFFIN** BOOK